MADE SIMPLE™
MEAL PREP
PLAN • SHOP • COOK

pil

Publications International, Ltd.

Microwave Cooking: Microwave ovens vary in wattage. Use the cooking times as guidelines and check for doneness before adding more time.

Let's get social!
 @Publications_International
 @PublicationsInternational
www.pilbooks.com

YOUR GUIDE TO MEAL PREP

WHAT IS MEAL PREP?

Easily stated, meal prep is the process of planning, preparing and storing of meals and/or snacks in advance. Meal prep can be done once per week or every few days depending on individual schedules and needs. You may think it takes a lot of time, but you'll be pleasantly surprised that you'll end up having more time during the week, if you prep properly.

THERE ARE SEVERAL TYPES OF MEAL PREP

MAKE-AHEAD MEALS: Preparing an entire meal and storing it for future use.

MAKE ONCE, EAT TWICE OR MORE: Making extra portions or double batches and freezing some for a later date. Or using leftovers for dinner the next night.

BATCH COOKING AND FREEZING: Preparing extra or multiple meals for portioning and freezing to use at a later time.

ONE-MEAL-AT-TIME: Preparing meals then portioning out multiple single meals in single-serve containers to be consumed within a few days.

PREPPING INGREDIENTS: Chopping and pre-portioning items ahead of time so they're ready to prepare when you are.

BENEFITS OF MEAL PREPPING

Of course, planning meals is going to benefit anyone who tries it. There's no doubt that last minute cooking results in meals that may be nutritionally unbalanced, meals that may cost more, and those that aren't as tasty. Who doesn't love a homemade meal over one that's quickly picked up or thrown together?

SAVING TIME/MONEY/WASTE: You'll plan what you need to buy, save money by repurposing items, and find ways to use up leftovers. Plus, you'll avoid excess impulse buying.

BALANCING MEALS AND PORTION CONTROL: You'll keep portions in line by preparing a variety of foods from all the food groups. It's so much more appealing to see a brightly, planned out, colorful collection of foods on the dinner plate like stir-fried chicken and vegetables with rice rather than a monotone plate of chicken tenders and French fries.

WEIGHT MANAGEMENT: Pre-planned and pre-portioned meals help avoid excess weight gain. Plus, knowing that the meals are prepared and waiting for you, it's less likely you'll pick up a snack on the way home from work or drive through a fast food restaurant to grab a quick, and not-so-nutritious, bite.

REDUCES STRESS WHEN TRYING TO FEED YOUR FAMILY LAST MINUTE: Your stress level will be reduced knowing meals are almost ready to eat, and therefore you won't find yourself searching your pantry and refrigerator in order to pull together a last-minute combination of what's on hand.

GETS EVERYONE INVOLVED: Everyone in the household should have specific tasks to help. Whether it's picking the recipes, keeping lists, helping shop or prep—when others help it gives them more responsibility. Not only do family members take more pride in the foods created, but in the case with kids, they're more likely to eat what they've helped prepare.

CREATE A PLAN

START SIMPLE. Keep foods simple and choose recipes you actually will enjoy and eat. Decide which foods you'll want to prep for the week. Start with collecting your favorite recipes, then plan what you'd like to make for dinners. If it's easiest for you, create a theme for each day. (You could go with Meatless Mondays, Taco Tuesdays, Kids' Choice Wednesday, etc., or chicken on Monday, ground beef on Tuesday, etc.) Then try extending it out to a 3- to 4-week cycle menu down the road. This helps to select meals your family likes, while keeping your shopping and recipe list workable for you.

CHOOSE A DAY TO SHOP AND PREP. Most grocery store specials and ads are distributed toward the end of the week, like Wednesdays and Thursdays. Keep your eyes open for what's on sale, and work your meals or sides around that. If you find that chicken breasts or fish fillets are on sale, stock up on them and store in the freezer until you need them. There's nothing better than saving money, while getting the foods you enjoy.

USE YOUR FREEZER. Make room in your freezer. Store whatever you can to help down the road. Whether you stock up on meats and chicken, frozen fruits and vegetables, bread dough, or use the freezer as a place to store cooked foods for later use, utilize it as best you can (see **chart** on page 6 for guidelines on best use of your freezer and refrigerator).

STOCK UP YOUR PANTRY. Of course, keeping staples on hand is key to smart meal prepping. Take time to organize your pantry so you can find what you need when you need it (see **chart** on page 8).

STORE FOODS PROPERLY. It's imperative that you store foods properly and in quality food containers or freezer bags at proper temperatures to keep as them as safe and flavorful as they can be. Most foods will keep about 3 to 5 days in the refrigerator. If you want to stretch your foods longer, you may choose to freeze some, too. Just be sure to thaw foods in the refrigerator ahead of time. Proper storage containers help maintain the flavor of the food and keep its color and texture intact. Make sure containers seal tightly and avoid any exposure to air—this can reduce the quality and texture of the food stored. Label your foods when you pack them up. You may think you'll remember what you stored, but as you add more items to your freezer or refrigerator, you may soon forget. Get proper labels and marking pens to jot down the food inside, plus be sure to date the label as well.

HAVE FUN WITH FOODS. Meal prepping can be a fun project for your family. Let kids help with menus, recipes, and prepping. These are memories and good times you'll cherish for years.

FREEZER AND REFRIGERATOR STORAGE GUIDELINES*

BREADS AND PASTRIES	FREEZER STORAGE	REFRIGERATOR STORAGE**
Baked breads/cookies	3 months	
Cakes/pastries	3 months	
Muffins/quick breads	3 months	
Pancakes/waffles	3 months	
MEAT/POULTRY/FISH	FREEZER STORAGE	REFRIGERATOR STORAGE**
Chicken/turkey (whole)	1 year	1–2 days
Chicken/turkey (cuts)	6–9 months	1–2 days
Ground chicken/turkey/beef	3–4 months	1–2 days
Beef/pork steaks	3–4 months	3–5 days
Lamb/veal roasts	4–12 months	3–5 days
Ham	2 months	3–4 days
Pork chops	4–6 months	3–5 days
Bacon/sausage	1–2 months	1 week
Cooked poultry dishes	4–6 months	3–4 days
Cooked meat	2–3 months	1–2 days
Lean fish (cod/flounder)	6–8 months	1–2 days
Fatty fish (trout/mackerel)	2–3 months	1–2 days
Cooked fish	4–6 months	1–2 days
Crab	10 months	2 days
Fresh shrimp/scallops	3–6 months	2 days
DAIRY	FREEZER STORAGE	REFRIGERATOR STORAGE**
Butter	6–9 months	3 months
Margarine	12 months	3 months
Cheese (hard/soft)	6 months	4 months
Yogurt/sour cream	Do not freeze	2–3 weeks
Cottage cheese	Do not freeze	1 week
Cream cheese	Do not freeze	2 months
MISCELLANEOUS	FREEZER STORAGE	REFRIGERATOR STORAGE**
Eggs	Do not freeze	3–5 weeks
Casseroles (cooked)	3 months	1–2 days
Rice/pasta (cooked)	3 months	2–3 days
FRUITS AND VEGETABLES	FREEZER STORAGE	REFRIGERATOR STORAGE**
Raw fruits	3–12 months	3–7 days
Raw vegetables	8–12 months	3–7 days

*This is just a guide for reference. Use your best judgement when storing foods. If you have doubts about the quality or smell of the food, discard it.
**Pay attention to expiration dates.

GETTING STARTED

SHOPPING LIST. Plan adequate time to shop. With list in hand take your time, and try to avoid impulse buying. Learn the layout of the grocery store so you'll know where to find items, thus getting in and out more quickly and efficiently. Every aspect of the grocery store layout is carefully planned—from the produce to the fresh meats to the dairy case. You'll notice that the fresh meats and dairy sections are most always in the far back of the store. This is done on purpose so walking through all the aisles becomes tempting and results in many impulse buys. The produce department is usually off to one side, whereas the aisles throughout the store carry packaged items and staples. Look up and down too. Popular items are placed at eye level to entice you, while many items that work just as well may be placed higher or lower on the shelves. With bakeries commonly in front, baked goods become tempting to hungry shoppers. And, of course, highlighted items sitting on end caps are there to grab your attention as you turn every corner. Merchandisers pay big bucks for all these placements.

BUY IN BULK. If you belong to a big box store, find items there that you can stock up on. Some can be a big bargain when purchased in larger portions. Whether it be multi-sized pounds of ground beef, salmon fillet, or chicken, you can easily break these down to smaller portions when you get home. Plus, big box stores offer good buys on staples like rice, quinoa, beans, and other grains, too!

PRE-PREP WHEN YOU CAN. When you return from the grocery, store the items you'll need in the next few days in the refrigerator. Chop up vegetables ahead of time, pre-package any large packages of meats, wash any fresh fruit, whatever you do now, helps save time later.

TO-GO CONTAINERS. Have your containers available before you start prepping. What type to choose? Bento boxes or Mason jars? Plastic or glass? Plastics are best for carrying in a bag or backpack. There are many styles available each differing in number of compartments. Glass, on the other hand are easier to clean but are heavier to lug around. And, then there are Mason jars—perfect for stacking foods, but again, heavy to carry. Of course, you'd probably want to avoid glass for your kids, so plastic may be a better bet. And, make sure you choose containers meant for food, are environmentally safe, and are leakproof.

PREP LIKE A PRO

Once you prep once or twice, you'll get the hang of it.

SCHEDULE YOUR PREP DAY. If the weekend works best for you, plan on it. Block out several hours, just like you're planning a meeting, and stick to it.

SORT OUT YOUR RECIPES. Plan which items take longer to prepare and others not so long. Assign tasks to family members.

DEFROST NECESSARY INGREDIENTS. Remove any frozen items from the freezer the night before you need them. Be sure to defrost your foods properly to avoid any food safety issues (see **chart** on page 9).

GET INGREDIENTS READY. Take all items you need out of the refrigerator and pantry.

PREPARE, PACK UP, LABEL AND STORE. You're on your way to cooking, packing, labeling and storing.

PANTRY STAPLES CHART*

IN THE REFRIGERATOR

PRODUCE

- Carrots
- Celery
- Garlic
- Lemons/limes
- Onions
- Potatoes
- Sweet potatoes
- Tomatoes

DAIRY

- Butter
- Eggs
- Cream cheese
- Shredded cheese (Cheddar and Mozzarella)
- Parmesan cheese
- Milk
- Yogurt

CONDIMENTS

- Mayonnaise
- Dijon mustard
- Honey
- Ketchup
- Peanut butter
- Soy sauce
- Worcestershire sauce
- Barbecue sauce
- Teriyaki sauce

IN THE FREEZER

MEAT/FISH

- Bacon
- Chicken breasts, thighs, legs, wings
- Ground turkey
- Ground beef
- Pork tenderloin/ pork cutlets
- Sausages (turkey, chicken, sweet Italian)
- Salmon fillets
- Tilapia fillets
- Shrimp

BREADS/BAGELS

- Bagels

VEGETABLES

- Frozen vegetables
- Frozen fruits

IN THE PANTRY

PASTA/RICE/GRAINS

- Spaghetti and pasta in variety of shapes and sizes
- Long-grain and short-grain rice
- Quinoa
- Assorted crackers

CANNED/BOXED GOODS

- Beans (white, black, kidney)
- Tomato sauce/paste
- Spaghetti sauce
- Canned tomatoes
- Broth (vegetable, chicken and beef)
- Canned tuna and salmon
- Canned/packaged fruits
- Canned vegetables

BAKING ITEMS

- Flour (white and whole wheat)
- Baking soda
- Baking powder
- Cornstarch
- Granulated sugar
- Brown sugar
- Powdered sugar

OIL/VINEGAR/WINE/SPICES

- Oil (vegetable, sesame and olive)
- Nonstick cooking spray
- Red and white wine vinegar
- Rice vinegar
- Balsamic vinegar
- Salt (table and Kosher), black and red pepper
- Bay leaves
- Chili powder
- Ground cumin
- Garlic powder and onion powder
- Dry mustard
- Dried oregano
- Dried basil
- Dried parsley
- Paprika
- Dried rosemary
- Dried thyme
- Bread crumbs (plain and seasoned)
- Dry white wine

This is just a guide. Use your own personal preferences and recipes to help you create your own pantry list.

RECIMES

We've created a collection of chapters to provide you with ideas to start you off and keep you going.

MAKE-AHEAD CASSEROLES: prepare in advance, ready to heat and eat when you are

HALF HOMEMADE: halfway to dinner, your meal will be ready in no time

COOK ONCE EAT TWICE: make a little extra, add a few ingredients and a second meal is on the way

SUPER EASY SANDWICHES: perfect for a quick meal anytime

SHEET PAN & ONE-POT DINNERS: prepare the entire meal on one pan—so easy

PACKABLE SALADS: make and take with you anytime, anywhere

GRAB-AND-GO BREAKFASTS: great choices for busy families

READY-TO-EAT SWEETS: everyone's favorite—for snacking or desserts

THREE WAYS TO SAFELY DEFROST MEAT

IN THE REFRIGERATOR

Refrigerator temperature should be between 34° and 40°F.

Place a plate or pan under the frozen meat to contain drippings as it defrosts.

Once defrosted, meat should be used within 1-2 days.

IN THE MICROWAVE

Place meat on microwavable plate, removing all store packaging or wrapping.

Defrost meats on LOW power or DEFROST cycle, in order to make sure inside of the meat is reached.

Cook meat promptly after defrosting.

IN COLD WATER BATH

Place frozen meat in a resealable, leak-proof bag.

Submerge meat in COLD water, changing water every 30 minutes.

Cook meat promptly after defrosting.

page 35

page 73

MAKE-AHEAD CASSEROLES

chapter one

Spend 30 minutes to an hour preparing a casserole on
the weekend and have a super easy dinner ready to go for
a night during the week. Most casseroles can be made ahead
of time and refrigerated or frozen until you need it. And as long
as you're making one, you might as well make two and freeze
one for later in a freezer- and oven-safe baking dish. Casseroles
also make great lunches. They transport easily in food storage
containers and reheat in minutes in the microwave.

CLASSIC LASAGNA

makes 6 to 8 servings

1 tablespoon olive oil	2 teaspoons Italian seasoning
8 ounces bulk mild Italian sausage	1 egg
8 ounces ground beef	1 container (15 ounces) ricotta cheese
1 medium onion, chopped	¾ cup grated Parmesan cheese, divided
3 cloves garlic, minced, divided	½ cup minced fresh parsley
1½ teaspoons salt, divided	¼ teaspoon black pepper
1 can (28 ounces) crushed tomatoes	12 uncooked no-boil lasagna noodles
1 can (28 ounces) diced tomatoes	4 cups (16 ounces) shredded mozzarella

1 Preheat oven to 350°F. Spray 13×9-inch baking dish with nonstick cooking spray.

2 Heat oil in large saucepan over medium-high heat. Add sausage, beef, onion, 2 cloves garlic and 1 teaspoon salt; cook and stir 10 minutes or until meat is no longer pink, breaking up meat with wooden spoon. Add tomatoes and Italian seasoning; bring to a boil. Reduce heat to medium-low; cook 15 minutes, stirring occasionally.

3 Meanwhile, beat egg in medium bowl. Stir in ricotta, ½ cup Parmesan, parsley, remaining 1 clove garlic, ½ teaspoon salt and pepper until well blended.

4 Spread ¼ cup sauce in prepared baking dish. Top with 3 noodles, breaking to fit if necessary. Spread one third of ricotta mixture over noodles. Sprinkle with 1 cup mozzarella; top with 2 cups sauce. Repeat layers of noodles, ricotta mixture, mozzarella and sauce two times. Top with remaining 3 noodles, sauce, 1 cup mozzarella and ¼ cup Parmesan. Cover dish with foil sprayed with cooking spray.

5 Bake 30 minutes. Remove foil; bake 10 to 15 minutes or until hot and bubbly. Let stand 10 minutes before serving.

TIP: The lasagna can be made ahead through step 4. Cover tightly with plastic wrap instead of foil and refrigerate up to 24 hours or freeze 1 month. Let refrigerated lasagna stand at room temperature 1 hour before baking; thaw frozen lasagna in the refrigerator 1 day and then let stand at room temperature 1 hour before baking. Remove plastic wrap and cover with greased foil just before baking.

FAMILY-STYLE FRANKFURTERS WITH RICE AND RED BEANS

makes 6 servings

1 tablespoon vegetable oil

1 onion, chopped

½ green bell pepper, chopped

2 cloves garlic, minced

1 can (about 15 ounces) red kidney beans, rinsed and drained

1 can (about 15 ounces) Great Northern beans, rinsed and drained

½ pound beef frankfurters, cut into ¼-inch-thick pieces

1 cup uncooked instant brown rice

1 cup vegetable broth

¼ cup packed brown sugar

¼ cup ketchup

3 tablespoons molasses

1 tablespoon Dijon mustard

1 Preheat oven to 350°F. Spray 13×9-inch baking dish with nonstick cooking spray.

2 Heat oil in large saucepan over medium-high heat. Add onion, bell pepper and garlic; cook and stir 2 minutes or until tender.

3 Add beans, frankfurters, rice, broth, brown sugar, ketchup, molasses and mustard to saucepan; gently stir until blended. Transfer to prepared baking dish.

4 Cover and bake 30 minutes or until rice is tender.

TIP: To make this casserole ahead of time, cook the vegetables as directed in step 2. Stir in everything as directed in step 3 except the broth and the rice. Place the mixture in the prepared baking dish, cover and refrigerate up to 1 day. Take the baking dish out of the refrigerator while you're preheating the oven. Stir in the rice and broth and bake about 30 minutes until the rice is tender.

REUBEN NOODLE BAKE

makes 6 servings

8 ounces uncooked egg noodles

5 ounces thinly sliced deli-style corned beef

2 cups (8 ounces) shredded Swiss cheese

1 can (about 14 ounces) sauerkraut with caraway seeds, drained

½ cup Thousand Island dressing

½ cup milk

1 tablespoon prepared mustard

2 slices pumpernickel bread

1 tablespoon butter, melted

1 Preheat oven to 350°F. Spray 13×9-inch baking dish with nonstick cooking spray. Cook noodles according to package directions; drain.

2 Meanwhile, cut corned beef into bite-size pieces. Combine noodles, corned beef, cheese and sauerkraut in prepared baking dish.

3 Combine dressing, milk and mustard in small bowl. Spoon evenly over noodle mixture.

4 Tear bread into large pieces; process in food processor or blender until crumbs form. Add butter; pulse to combine. Sprinkle over casserole.

5 Bake 25 to 30 minutes or until heated through.

TIP: Prepare casserole through step 4. Cover and refrigerate up to 1 day. Let the casserole stand at room temperature while the oven is preheating. Remove cover. Bake about 30 minutes or until heated through.

BAKED PASTA WITH RICOTTA

makes 12 servings

1 package (16 ounces) uncooked
  rigatoni or penne pasta

2 eggs

1 container (15 ounces) ricotta cheese

⅔ cup grated Parmesan cheese

½ teaspoon salt

⅛ teaspoon black pepper

2 jars (26 ounces each) marinara sauce,
  divided

3 cups (12 ounces) shredded mozzarella
  cheese, divided

1 Preheat oven to 375°F. Spray 13×9-inch baking dish with nonstick cooking spray.

2 Cook rigatoni in large saucepan of boiling salted water until al dente according to package directions; drain and return to saucepan. Meanwhile, whisk eggs in medium bowl. Stir in ricotta, Parmesan, salt and pepper until well blended.

3 Spread 2 cups marinara sauce over bottom of prepared dish; spoon half of cooked pasta over sauce. Top with half of ricotta mixture and 1 cup mozzarella. Repeat layers of marinara sauce, pasta and ricotta mixture. Top with 1 cup mozzarella, remaining marinara sauce and 1 cup mozzarella.

4 Cover with foil; bake about 1 hour or until bubbly. Uncover and bake about 5 minutes more or until cheese is completely melted. Let stand 15 minutes before serving.

TIP: This casserole can be made ahead through step 4. Cover tightly with plastic wrap instead of foil and refrigerate up to 24 hours or freeze 1 month. Let refrigerated casserole stand at room temperature 1 hour before baking; thaw frozen casserole in the refrigerator 1 day and then let stand at room temperature 1 hour before baking. Remove plastic wrap and cover with greased foil just before baking.

KALE, GORGONZOLA & NOODLE CASSEROLE

makes 6 servings

- 6 ounces uncooked rotini or egg noodles
- 1 large bunch kale, stems removed, coarsely chopped (about 8 cups)
- 2 tablespoons butter
- 1 clove garlic, smashed
- ¼ cup chopped green onions
- 2 tablespoons all-purpose flour
- 2¼ cups half-and-half
- 4 ounces gorgonzola cheese, crumbled
- 4 ounces fontina cheese, cut into small chunks
- ½ teaspoon salt
- ¼ teaspoon black pepper
- ¼ teaspoon ground nutmeg
- ¼ cup panko bread crumbs

1 Preheat oven to 350°F. Spray 9-inch square baking dish with nonstick cooking spray. Cook noodles according to package directions in large saucepan of boiling salted water until al dente. Drain and return to saucepan.

2 Meanwhile, place kale in large saucepan with 1 inch water. Cover; bring to a simmer. Steam kale 15 minutes or until tender. Drain well, pressing out excess liquid, and set aside.

3 Melt butter in large saucepan or deep skillet over medium-low heat. Add garlic and green onions; cook and stir over low heat 5 minutes. Discard garlic. Whisk in flour until paste forms. Gradually add half-and-half, stirring frequently, until mixture thickens. Gradually add cheeses until melted. Stir in salt, pepper and nutmeg. Stir in noodles and kale; mix well. Spoon into prepared baking dish. Sprinkle with panko.

4 Bake 30 minutes or until sauce is bubbly and top is lightly browned.

TIP: Prepare casserole through step 3. Cover and refrigerate up to 1 day. Let the casserole stand at room temperature while the oven is preheating. Remove cover. Bake about 30 minutes or until heated through.

MAKE AHEAD • ONE DISH

TUSCAN BAKED RIGATONI

makes 6 to 8 servings

1 package (16 ounces) rigatoni pasta

1 pound bulk Italian sausage

2 cups (8 ounces) shredded fontina cheese

2 tablespoons olive oil

2 bulbs fennel, thinly sliced

4 cloves garlic, minced

1 can (28 ounces) crushed tomatoes

1 cup whipping cream

1 teaspoon salt

1 teaspoon black pepper

8 cups packed fresh spinach

1 can (about 15 ounces) cannellini beans, rinsed and drained

2 tablespoons pine nuts

½ cup grated Parmesan cheese

1 Preheat oven to 350°F. Spray 4-quart baking dish with nonstick cooking spray. Cook pasta according to package directions in large saucepan of boiling salted water until al dente; drain and return to saucepan.

2 Brown sausage in large skillet over medium-high heat, stirring to break up meat; drain fat. Transfer sausage to prepared baking dish. Add rigatoni and fontina cheese; mix well.

3 Heat oil in same skillet; add fennel and garlic. Cook and stir over medium heat 3 minutes or until fennel is crisp-tender. Add tomatoes, cream, salt and pepper; cook and stir until slightly thickened. Stir in spinach, beans and pine nuts; cook until heated through.

4 Pour sauce mixture over pasta mixture; toss to coat. Transfer to prepared baking dish; sprinkle evenly with Parmesan cheese. Bake 30 minutes or until bubbly and heated through.

TIP: To make this casserole vegetarian, use vegetarian Italian sausage. Slice it ½ inch thick and cook it in a nonstick skillet in a teaspoon of olive oil until browned around edges. Proceed with the rest of the recipe as directed. Or you can omit the sausage altogether.

MAKE-AHEAD CASSEROLES   23

MEXICAN RICE OLÉ

makes 4 servings

1 teaspoon vegetable oil

1 cup uncooked long grain rice

1 teaspoon salt

1 clove garlic, minced

1 can (about 14 ounces) chicken or vegetable broth

¼ cup water

1 can (10¾ ounces) condensed cream of chicken or celery soup, undiluted

¾ cup sour cream

1 can (4 ounces) chopped mild green chiles, undrained

⅓ cup salsa

1 teaspoon ground cumin

1 cup (4 ounces) shredded Cheddar cheese

1 can (about 2 ounces) sliced black olives, drained

1 Preheat oven to 350°F. Spray 3-quart baking dish with nonstick cooking spray.

2 Heat oil in large skillet over medium heat. Add rice, salt and garlic; cook and stir 2 to 3 minutes or until rice is well coated. Pour broth and water into skillet; cook about 15 minutes or until rice is tender, stirring occasionally.

3 Remove skillet from heat. Stir in soup, sour cream, chiles, salsa and cumin; mix well. Transfer to prepared baking dish.

4 Bake 20 minutes. Top with cheese and olives; bake 5 to 10 minutes or until cheese is melted and casserole is heated through.

TIP: To make ahead of time, prepare through step 3. Remove from the refrigerator while the oven preheats. To make this casserole a heartier meal, add 1 cup chopped cooked chicken or pork to the rice mixture. Serve it with a packaged Southwestern salad kit.

TUNA TOMATO CASSEROLE

makes 6 servings

2 cans (6 ounces each) tuna, drained and flaked

1 cup mayonnaise

1 onion, finely chopped

¼ teaspoon salt

¼ teaspoon black pepper

1 package (12 ounces) wide egg noodles, uncooked

8 to 10 plum tomatoes, sliced ¼ inch thick

1 cup (4 ounces) shredded Cheddar or mozzarella cheese

1 Preheat oven to 375°F.

2 Combine tuna, mayonnaise, onion, salt and pepper in medium bowl; mix well.

3 Cook noodles in large saucepan of boiling salted water according to package directions until al dente; drain and return to saucepan. Gently stir in tuna mixture until well blended. Layer half of noodle mixture, half of tomatoes and half of cheese in 13×9-inch baking dish; press down slightly. Repeat layers.

4 Bake 20 minutes or until cheese is melted and casserole is heated through.

TIP: To make ahead of time, prepare through step 3. Cover and refrigerate until needed, and remove from the refrigerator while the oven preheats.

BAKED PASTA CASSEROLE

makes 6 servings

1 package (16 ounces) uncooked wagon wheel (rotelle) pasta

1 pound ground beef

1 small yellow onion, chopped

½ green bell pepper, chopped

2 cloves garlic, minced

2 cups pasta sauce
  Black pepper

1 cup (4 ounces) shredded Italian-style mozzarella and Parmesan cheese blend

1 Preheat oven to 350°F. Cook pasta according to package directions in large saucepan of boiling salted water until al dente; drain and return to saucepan.

2 Meanwhile, heat medium nonstick skillet over medium-high heat. Add beef, onion, bell pepper and garlic; cook and stir 6 to 8 minutes or until beef is no longer pink and vegetables are crisp-tender, breaking up meat with wooden spoon. Drain fat.

3 Add beef mixture, pasta sauce and black pepper to pasta in saucepan; mix well. Spoon mixture into 3-quart baking dish. Sprinkle with cheese.

4 Bake 15 minutes or until heated through.

TIP: To make ahead, assemble casserole as directed above through step 3. Cover and refrigerate several hours or overnight. Bake, uncovered, in preheated 350°F oven 30 minutes or until heated through.

HALF HOMEMADE

chapter two

A supermarket rotisserie chicken can be a weeknight cook's best friend. Pantry staples and other convenience products like refrigerated dough, packaged tortellini and biscuit dough also make dinner and meal prep easier.

CHICKEN AND GNOCCHI SOUP

makes 6 to 8 servings (9 cups)

- ¼ cup (½ stick) butter
- 1 tablespoon olive oil
- 1 cup finely diced onion
- 2 stalks celery, finely chopped
- 2 cloves garlic, minced
- ¼ cup all-purpose flour
- 4 cups half-and-half
- 1 can (about 14 ounces) chicken broth
- 1 teaspoon salt
- ½ teaspoon dried thyme

- ½ teaspoon dried parsley flakes
- ¼ teaspoon ground nutmeg
- 1 package (about 16 ounces) uncooked gnocchi
- 1 package (6 ounces) fully cooked chicken strips, chopped or 1 cup diced cooked chicken
- 1 cup shredded carrots
- 1 cup coarsely chopped fresh spinach

1 Melt butter in large saucepan or Dutch oven over medium heat; add oil. Add onion, celery and garlic; cook about 8 minutes or until vegetables are softened and onion is translucent, stirring occasionally.

2 Whisk in flour; cook and stir about 1 minute. Whisk in half-and-half; cook about 15 minutes or until thickened, stirring occasionally.

3 Whisk in broth, salt, thyme, parsley flakes and nutmeg; cook 10 minutes or until soup is slightly thickened, stirring occasionally.

4 Add gnocchi, chicken, carrots and spinach; cook about 5 minutes or until gnocchi are heated through.

TIP: To make this soup ahead of time, prepare it through step 3, transfer it to a large jar or food storage container and let it cool to room temperature. Store the soup in the refrigerator for a day or two. Transfer it to a large saucepan and reheat gently over medium heat (do not boil), whisking frequently. When the soup is hot, proceed with step 4, adding additional broth or half-and-half to thin to desired consistency.

BEEF AND VEGGIE FLATBREAD

— makes 4 servings —

8 ounces ground beef

1 clove garlic, minced

1 loaf (11 ounces) refrigerated French bread dough

½ cup tomato sauce, pizza sauce or marinara sauce

1 teaspoon dried oregano

¼ teaspoon red pepper flakes (optional)

12 slices (about ¾ ounce) turkey pepperoni, halved

½ cup sliced mushrooms

½ cup thinly sliced green bell pepper

½ cup thinly sliced yellow onion

¼ cup chopped fresh basil

1 cup (4 ounces) shredded mozzarella cheese

2 teaspoons grated Parmesan cheese

1 Preheat oven to 425°F.

2 Spray medium nonstick skillet with nonstick cooking spray; heat over medium-high heat. Add beef and garlic; cook 6 to 8 minutes or until beef is no longer pink, breaking up beef with wooden spoon. Drain fat.

3 Spray large baking sheets with nonstick cooking spray. Unroll dough on work surface. Cut into 4 pieces; place on prepared baking sheets.

4 Spread tomato sauce evenly over dough. Sprinkle with oregano and red pepper flakes, if desired. Top with pepperoni, beef, mushrooms, bell pepper, onion, basil and mozzarella cheese. Bake 10 minutes or until golden brown on edges. Sprinkle with Parmesan cheese.

TIP: Wrap leftovers in foil and refrigerate. Reheat in toaster oven or regular oven until heated through.

PROSCIUTTO, ASPARAGUS AND CHICKEN PIZZA

makes 4 servings

1 package (10 ounces) prepared whole wheat pizza crust (12 inches)

½ cup pizza sauce

4 asparagus spears, cut into 1-inch pieces

½ cup chopped prosciutto*

½ cup chopped red onion

1 cup shredded cooked chicken

1 cup (4 ounces) finely shredded mozzarella cheese

*You can find chopped prosciutto in the deli section of the supermarket.

1 Preheat oven to 450°F. Place pizza crust on baking sheet. Spread pizza sauce on crust and arrange asparagus, prosciutto, onion and chicken on top. Sprinkle evenly with cheese.

2 Bake 10 to 12 minutes or until cheese is melted and crust is browned.

TIP: Prepared pizza crust and cooked chicken make a super easy dinner, and this recipe can be a formula for many easy dinners. Substitute any cooked protein for the chicken, bacon for the prosciutto and any vegetables for the asparagus and onion.

SOFT CHICKEN TACOS

makes 4 servings

8 (6- or 7-inch) corn tortillas

2 tablespoons butter

1 medium onion, chopped

1½ cups shredded cooked chicken

1 can (4 ounces) diced mild green chiles, drained

2 tablespoons chopped fresh cilantro

1 cup sour cream

Salt and black pepper

1½ cups (6 ounces) shredded Monterey Jack cheese

1 large avocado, sliced

Green taco sauce

1 Preheat oven to 350°F. Stack and wrap tortillas in foil. Bake 15 minutes or until heated through.

2 Melt butter in large skillet over medium heat. Add onion; cook until tender. Add chicken, chiles and cilantro; cook and stir 3 minutes or until mixture is hot. Reduce heat to low. Stir in sour cream; season with salt and black pepper. Cook and stir until heated through; do not boil.

3 To assemble tacos, spoon about 3 tablespoons chicken mixture into center of each tortilla; sprinkle with 2 tablespoons cheese. Top with avocado; drizzle with taco sauce. Sprinkle tacos with remaining cheese. Roll tortilla into cone shape or fold in half.

TIP: To make these easy tacos into a quick complete dinner, serve with a prepared package of Spanish rice and warmed canned refried beans.

PEPPER PITA PIZZAS

makes 4 servings

1 teaspoon olive oil

1 medium onion, thinly sliced

1 medium red bell pepper, cut into thin strips

1 medium green bell pepper, cut into thin strips

4 cloves garlic, minced

2 tablespoons minced fresh basil or 2 teaspoons dried basil

1 tablespoon minced fresh oregano or 1 teaspoon dried oregano

2 Italian plum tomatoes, coarsely chopped

4 (6-inch) pita breads

1 cup (4 ounces) shredded Monterey Jack cheese

1 Preheat oven to 425°F.

2 Heat oil in medium nonstick skillet over medium heat until hot. Add onion, bell peppers, garlic, basil and oregano. Partially cover; cook 5 minutes or until tender, stirring occasionally. Add tomatoes. Partially cover and cook 3 minutes.

3 Place pita rounds on baking sheet. Divide tomato mixture evenly among pitas; top each pita with ¼ cup cheese. Bake 5 minutes or until cheese is melted.

TIP: Pita bread makes a perfect (and super easy) pizza crust in minutes. You could also substitute flour tortillas for the pitas. For a cheesy stuffed crust, split the pita in half crosswise to form two thin layers. Sprinkle one layer with ¼ cup cheese and top with the other layers. Proceed with steps 2 and 3.

QUESADILLA GRANDE

makes 1 serving

2 (8-inch) flour tortillas

2 to 3 large fresh stemmed spinach leaves

½ cup shredded cooked chicken

2 tablespoons salsa

1 tablespoon chopped fresh cilantro

¼ cup (1 ounce) shredded Monterey Jack cheese

2 teaspoons vegetable oil

1 Place one tortilla on work surface; top evenly with spinach. Place chicken in single layer over spinach. Spoon salsa over chicken. Sprinkle with cilantro; top with cheese. Place remaining tortilla on top, pressing tortilla down so filling becomes compact.

2 Heat 1 teaspoon oil in large nonstick skillet over medium heat. Place quesadilla in skillet. Cook 4 to 5 minutes or until bottom tortilla is lightly browned. Slide tortilla onto cutting board; carefully turn over. Heat remaining 1 teaspoon oil in skillet; add tortilla, uncooked side down. Cook 4 minutes or until bottom tortilla is browned and cheese is melted. Cut in half to serve.

TIP: To have leftover quesadillas for lunch, wrap cooked tortilla in foil Reheat in foil in toaster oven or preheated 375°F oven.

PEPPERONI PIZZA BAGELS

makes 4 servings

4 sesame seed bagels

¼ cup marinara sauce

¼ cup mini pepperoni slices

¼ cup (1 ounce) shredded mozzarella cheese

Dried oregano

1 Preheat oven or toaster oven to 350°F. Cut bagels in half lengthwise. Top each with sauce, pepperoni and cheese.

2 Place bagels on baking sheet. Bake 7 to 10 minutes or until cheese is melted and browned. Sprinkle with oregano.

TIP: This is a great recipe to use up leftover bagels. Make extra pizza bagels to pack for lunch—they're good both cold and reheated in a toaster oven or microwave.

CHICKEN BACON QUESADILLAS

makes 4 servings

- 4 teaspoons vegetable oil, divided
- 4 (8-inch) flour tortillas
- 1 cup (4 ounces) shredded Colby-Jack cheese
- 2 cups coarsely chopped cooked chicken
- 4 slices bacon, crisp-cooked and coarsely chopped
- ½ cup pico de gallo, plus additional for serving
- Sour cream and guacamole (optional)

1 Heat large nonstick skillet over medium heat; brush with 1 teaspoon oil. Place one tortilla in skillet; sprinkle with ¼ cup cheese. Spread ½ cup chicken over one half of tortilla; top with one fourth of bacon and 2 tablespoons pico de gallo.

2 Cook 1 to 2 minutes or until cheese is melted and bottom of tortilla is lightly browned. Fold tortilla over filling, pressing with spatula. Transfer to cutting board; cool slightly. Cut into wedges. Repeat with remaining ingredients. Serve with additional pico de gallo, sour cream and guacamole, if desired.

SUPER FAST BAGELS

makes 4 servings

1 cup self-rising flour
1 cup plain nonfat Greek yogurt
1 large egg, beaten

Sesame seeds, poppy seeds, dried onion flakes, everything bagel seasoning (optional)
Cream cheese or butter (optional)

1 Preheat oven to 400°F. Line baking sheet with parchment paper.

2 Combine flour and yogurt in large bowl; mix well with wooden spoon. Place dough on lightly floured surface; knead 4 to 5 minutes or until dough is smooth and elastic. Shape dough into a ball.

3 Cut into four equal portions. Roll into balls. Pull and stretch dough to create ring shape, inserting finger into center to create hole. Place on prepared baking sheet; brush with egg wash. Sprinkle with desired toppings.

4 Bake 15 minutes or until lightly browned. Remove to wire rack; cool slightly. Serve with cream cheese, if desired.

TIP: If you don't have self-rising flour, whisk 1 cup all-purpose flour, 1½ teaspoons baking powder and ½ teaspoon salt in small bowl until well blended. Use as directed in step 2.

COOK ONCE EAT TWICE

This chapter provides pairs of recipes that allow you to cook one big meal and use leftovers to cook a second, quick and easy meal the next night. For example, on the first night cook spaghetti and meatballs with extra meatballs. Then on the second night, reheat the extra meatballs and sauce, put them on bread with cheese, and just like that you have meatball subs.

CLASSIC MACARONI AND CHEESE

makes 4 servings plus leftovers for Mac and Cheese Pizza

2 cups uncooked elbow macaroni

¼ cup (½ stick) butter

¼ cup all-purpose flour

2½ cups whole milk

1 teaspoon salt

⅛ teaspoon black pepper

4 cups (16 ounces) shredded Colby-Jack cheese

1 Cook pasta in large saucepan of boiling salted water according to package directions until al dente; drain and return to saucepan.

2 Melt butter in another large saucepan over medium heat. Add flour; whisk until well blended and bubbly. Gradually add milk, salt and pepper, whisking until blended. Cook and stir until milk begins to bubble. Add cheese, 1 cup at a time; cook and stir until cheese is melted and sauce is smooth.

3 Add cooked pasta to saucepan; stir gently until blended. Cook until heated through.

TIP: This recipe makes 8 cups, enough for 8 servings, or 4 servings plus 4 cups leftovers for Mac and Cheese Pizza on page 55 or Chili Mac on page 89.

ONE DISH • QUICK & EASY

MAC AND CHEESE PIZZA

makes 4 to 6 servings

4 cups leftover macaroni and cheese from Classic Macaroni and Cheese (page 53)
1 tablespoon olive oil
1 cup sliced mushrooms
8 ounces uncooked sweet Italian sausage
1 cup marinara sauce
1 cup (4 ounces) shredded mozzarella cheese

1 Preheat oven to 350°F. Spray 10-inch round deep-dish pizza pan, tart pan or shallow casserole with nonstick cooking spray. Press macaroni and cheese firmly into even layer in pan. Bake 15 minutes.

2 Meanwhile, heat oil in large skillet over medium heat. Add mushrooms; cook and stir 5 minutes, stirring occasionally. Increase heat to medium-high. Add sausage; cook until browned, breaking into bite-size pieces with wooden spoon. Drain fat. Stir in marinara sauce; cook 1 minute or until heated through.

3 Spread sauce mixture evenly over macaroni crust. Sprinkle with mozzarella cheese. Bake 15 to 20 minutes or until sauce is bubbly and cheese is melted. Let stand 5 minutes before slicing.

TIP: To make this recipe not using leftovers, follow the directions for Classic Macaroni and Cheese on page 53 but decrease all the ingredients by half. You can substitute shredded Cheddar cheese for the Colby-Jack or use a mix of Cheddar, Monterey Jack, Parmesan and fontina.

ROASTED CAULIFLOWER

—————— makes 4 servings with leftovers for Lemon Cream Pasta with Roasted Cauliflower ——————

2 heads cauliflower, broken into 1-inch florets

2 tablespoons olive oil

¾ teaspoon Italian seasoning (optional)

1 teaspoon salt

¼ teaspoon black pepper

1 Preheat oven to 425°F. Spray baking sheet with nonstick cooking spray.

2 Place cauliflower on prepared baking sheet. Drizzle with oil. Sprinkle evenly with Italian seasoning, if desired, salt and pepper. Gently toss; arrange in single layer.

3 Bake 35 to 45 minutes or until cauliflower is well browned and tender, stirring once.

TIP: Serve roasted cauliflower as a side dish to just about an meal. In addition to using it in the recipe on page 59, you could also add it to Classic Macaroni and Cheese (page 53), Baked Pasta with Ricotta (page 19) or Chickpea Tikka Masala (page 125).

LEMON CREAM PASTA WITH ROASTED CAULIFLOWER

makes 6 to 8 servings

8 ounces uncooked cavatappi pasta
  Leftover cauliflower from Roasted
    Cauliflower (page 57)
¼ cup (½ stick) butter, cut into pieces
¼ cup all-purpose flour
2 cups milk
½ teaspoon salt

⅛ teaspoon black pepper
½ cup shredded Parmesan cheese
  Grated peel and juice of 1 lemon
¼ cup chopped almonds, toasted
  Baby arugula
  Aleppo pepper or red pepper flakes
    (optional)

1 Cook pasta in large saucepan of boiling salted water according to package directions until al dente. Drain, reserving 1 cup pasta cooking water. Place pasta in large bowl; add cauliflower.

2 Melt butter in same saucepan over medium heat; whisk in flour until smooth paste forms. Whisk in milk, salt and black pepper; cook 2 to 3 minutes or until thickened. Whisk in ½ cup reserved pasta water and Parmesan until smooth. Pour over pasta and cauliflower; stir to coat. Add additional pasta water by tablespoonfuls to loosen sauce, if needed. Stir in lemon peel, lemon juice and almonds. Top with arugula or gently fold into pasta mixture. Sprinkle with Aleppo pepper, if desired.

MARINATED ITALIAN SAUSAGE AND PEPPERS

makes 4 servings plus leftovers for Sausage and Pepper Pizza

½ cup olive oil

¼ cup red wine vinegar

2 tablespoons chopped fresh parsley

1 tablespoon dried oregano

2 cloves garlic, crushed

1 teaspoon salt

1 teaspoon black pepper

6 links hot or sweet Italian sausage

2 red onions, cut into rings

4 bell peppers, cut into quarters
   Horseradish-Mustard Spread (recipe follows)

1 Combine oil, vinegar, parsley, oregano, garlic, salt and black pepper in small bowl. Place sausages, onions and bell peppers in large resealable food storage bag; pour oil mixture over sausage and vegetables. Seal bag; turn to coat. Marinate in refrigerator 1 to 2 hours.

2 Prepare Horseradish-Mustard Spread; set aside. Prepare grill for direct cooking.

3 Remove sausages, onions and bell peppers from marinade; reserve marinade. Grill sausage, covered, over medium heat 5 minutes. Turn sausages and place onions and bell peppers on grid; brush with reserved marinade. Discard remaining marinade. Grill, covered, 5 minutes or until sausages are cooked through and vegetables are crisp-tender. Serve sausages and vegetables with Horseradish-Mustard Spread.

HORSERADISH-MUSTARD SPREAD: Combine 3 tablespoons mayonnaise, 1 tablespoon chopped fresh parsley, 1 tablespoon prepared horseradish, 1 tablespoon Dijon mustard, 2 teaspoons garlic powder and 1 teaspoon black pepper in medium bowl. Mix well.

SAUSAGE AND PEPPER PIZZA

makes 4 servings

½ cup tomato sauce

1 clove garlic, minced

½ teaspoon dried basil

½ teaspoon dried oregano

⅛ teaspoon red pepper flakes (optional)

Grilled sausages from Marinated Italian Sausage and Peppers (page 61)

Grilled onion and bell peppers from Marinated Italian Sausage and Peppers (page 61)

1 (12-inch) prepared pizza crust

1½ cups (6 ounces) shredded fontina cheese or pizza cheese blend

½ cup grated Parmesan cheese

1 Preheat oven to 450°F. Combine tomato sauce, garlic, basil, oregano and red pepper flakes, if desired, in small bowl. Cut sausages in half lengthwise, then cut crosswise into ½-inch slices. Cut onion and bell peppers into 1-inch pieces.

2 Place pizza crust on pizza pan or baking sheet. Spread tomato sauce mixture over crust to within 1 inch of edge. Sprinkle fontina cheese over tomato sauce; top with sausage, onion and bell peppers. Sprinkle with Parmesan cheese.

3 Bake 12 minutes or until crust is crisp and cheeses are melted.

TIP: To save time, ½ cup pizza sauce may be substituted for the tomato sauce and seasonings.

LEMON-GARLIC SALMON WITH TZATZIKI SAUCE

makes 4 servings plus leftovers for Salmon Cakes

½ cup diced cucumber
1 teaspoon salt, divided
1 cup plain nonfat Greek yogurt
3 tablespoons fresh lemon juice, divided

1 teaspoon grated lemon peel, divided
1 teaspoon minced garlic, divided
¼ teaspoon black pepper
6 (6-ounce) skinless salmon fillets

1 Place cucumber in small colander set over small bowl; sprinkle with ¼ teaspoon salt. Drain 1 hour.

2 For tzatziki sauce, stir yogurt, cucumber, 1 tablespoon lemon juice, ½ teaspoon lemon peel, ½ teaspoon garlic and ¼ teaspoon salt in small bowl until combined. Cover and refrigerate until ready to use.

3 Combine remaining 2 tablespoons lemon juice, ½ teaspoon lemon peel, ½ teaspoon garlic, ½ teaspoon salt and pepper in small bowl; mix well. Rub evenly onto salmon.

4 Heat nonstick grill pan over medium-high heat. Cook salmon 5 minutes per side or until fish begins to flake when tested with fork. Wrap 2 fillets in plastic wrap for salmon cakes; refrigerate. Serve remaining salmon with sauce.

SALMON CAKES WITH CREAMY CAPER CHIVE SAUCE

makes 4 servings

- 2 slices whole wheat bread
- 2 egg whites, slightly beaten
- 2 leftover salmon fillets from Lemon-Garlic Salmon (page 65)
- 2 tablespoons chopped fresh chives, divided
- ¾ to 1 teaspoon Old Bay seasoning
- 2 teaspoons canola oil
- ¼ cup sour cream
- 1 tablespoon drained capers
  Lemon or lime wedges (optional)

1 Tear bread into pieces; place in bowl of food processor. Process until finely minced. Place in medium bowl; stir in egg whites. Break salmon into small chunks; add to bowl with 1 tablespoon chives and seasoning. Mix well. Shape into 4 patties about 3 inches in diameter and ½ inch thick.

2 Heat oil in large nonstick skillet over medium heat. Add salmon cakes; cook 3 to 4 minutes per side or until golden brown. Meanwhile, combine sour cream, remaining 1 tablespoon chives and capers in small bowl; mix well. Serve salmon cakes with caper sauce and lemon wedges, if desired.

TIP: To make this recipe on its own, use 1 can (14¾ ounces) sockeye salmon, drained, bones and skin discarded, instead of leftover salmon fillets.

SPAGHETTI AND MEATBALLS WITH RICOTTA

makes 4 servings plus leftovers for Speedy Meatball Subs

MEATBALLS

- 2 tablespoons olive oil
- ½ cup plain dry bread crumbs
- ½ cup milk
- 1 cup finely chopped yellow onion
- 2 green onions, finely chopped
- ½ cup grated Romano cheese
- 2 eggs, beaten
- ¼ cup finely chopped fresh parsley
- ¼ cup finely chopped fresh basil
- 2 cloves garlic, minced
- 2 teaspoons salt
- ¼ teaspoon black pepper
- 1 pound ground beef
- 1 pound ground pork

SAUCE

- 2 tablespoons olive oil
- 2 tablespoons butter
- 1 cup finely chopped yellow onion
- 1 clove garlic, minced
- 1 can (28 ounces) whole Italian plum tomatoes, coarsely chopped, juice reserved
- 1 can (28 ounces) crushed tomatoes
- 1 teaspoon salt
- ¼ teaspoon black pepper
- ¼ cup finely chopped fresh basil
- 1 to 1½ cups ricotta cheese
  Hot cooked spaghetti

1 Preheat oven to 375°F. Brush 2 tablespoons oil over large rimmed baking sheet.

2 Combine bread crumbs and milk in large bowl; mix well. Add 1 cup yellow onion, green onions, Romano, eggs, parsley, ¼ cup basil, 2 cloves garlic, 2 teaspoons salt and ¼ teaspoon black pepper; mix well. Add beef and pork; mix gently but thoroughly until blended. Shape mixture by 2 tablespoons into balls. Place meatballs on prepared baking sheet; turn to coat with oil.

3 Bake about 15 minutes or until meatballs are cooked through (165°F). Meanwhile, prepare sauce.

4 Heat 2 tablespoons oil and butter in large saucepan over medium heat until butter is melted. Add 1 cup yellow onion; cook 8 minutes or until tender and lightly browned, stirring frequently. Add 1 clove garlic; cook and stir 1 minute or until fragrant. Add plum tomatoes with juice, crushed tomatoes, 1 teaspoon salt and ¼ teaspoon black pepper; bring to a simmer. Reduce heat to medium-low; cook 20 minutes, stirring occasionally.

5 Stir ¼ cup basil into sauce. Add meatballs; cook 10 minutes, stirring occasionally. Transfer meatballs and sauce to serving dish; dollop tablespoonfuls of ricotta between meatballs. Serve with spaghetti.

SPEEDY MEATBALL SUBS

makes 4 to 5 servings

Leftover sauce and meatballs from Spaghetti and Meatballs with Ricotta (page 69)

4 to 5 sub or hoagie rolls, split
8 to 10 slices provolone cheese
Chopped fresh parsley (optional)

1 Preheat oven to 400°F. Line baking sheet with foil.

2 Reheat sauce and meatballs in microwave or large saucepan over medium heat.

3 Place rolls on prepared baking sheet. Bake 3 minutes or until lightly toasted.

4 Spoon sauce and meatballs on bottom halves of rolls; top with cheese slices (two per sandwich). Bake about 3 minutes or until cheese melts. Sprinkle with parsley, if desired; top with top halves of rolls.

TIP: To make this recipe on its own without leftovers, use 1 jar (24 ounces) of pasta sauce and 1 pound frozen Italian-style meatballs. Pour sauce into large saucepan; stir in meatballs. Heat over medium heat until meatballs are cooked through.

DILL-CRUSTED SALMON

makes 4 servings with leftovers for Garlic Bread and Salmon Salad

- 6 salmon fillets (about 6 ounces each)
- ¾ cup panko bread crumbs
- ½ cup finely chopped fresh dill
- ¼ cup mayonnaise
- 2 tablespoons olive oil
- 1 teaspoon salt
- ½ teaspoon red pepper flakes

1 Preheat oven to 400°F. Spray rack in roasting pan with nonstick cooking spray. Place salmon on rack.

2 Combine panko, dill, mayonnaise, oil, salt and red pepper flakes in medium bowl; mix well. Mound mixture evenly on top of salmon, pressing to adhere.

3 Bake 20 to 25 minutes or until topping is browned and fish begins to flake when tested with fork. Wrap 2 fillets in plastic wrap for Garlic Bread and Salmon Salad; serve remaining salmon immediately.

GARLIC BREAD AND SALMON SALAD

makes 4 servings

4 slices day-old light whole wheat bread

1 clove garlic, cut in half

2 leftover salmon fillets from Dill-Crusted Salmon (page 73)

¾ cup chopped green onions, green parts only

2 cups cherry or grape tomatoes, halved

2 tablespoons olive oil

3 tablespoons white wine vinegar

½ teaspoon salt

¼ teaspoon black pepper

¼ cup minced fresh basil

1 Preheat broiler. Set rack 3 to 4 inches from heat. Rub one side of each bread slice with garlic. Discard garlic. Set bread, garlic side up, on broiler rack. Broil 20 to 30 seconds or until lightly browned; watch carefully and remove when done to avoid burning.

2 Cut bread into 1-inch pieces when cool enough to handle.

3 Combine salmon, green onions and tomatoes in large serving bowl. Combine oil, vinegar, salt and pepper in small bowl. Pour over salmon mixture. Add garlic bread cubes and toss again. Sprinkle with basil.

TIP: To make this recipe on its own, use 1 can or pouch (7½ ounces) salmon, drained flaked, instead of leftover salmon fillets.

GARLIC SKEWERED SHRIMP

makes 4 servings with leftovers for Shrimp and Couscous Salad

2 pounds raw large shrimp, peeled and deveined

¼ cup soy sauce

2 tablespoons vegetable oil

4 cloves garlic, minced

¼ teaspoon red pepper flakes (optional)

3 green onions, cut into 1-inch pieces

Hot cooked rice

1 Prepare grill for direct cooking over medium heat. Soak 8 (12-inch) wooden skewers in hot water 30 minutes. Meanwhile, place shrimp in large resealable food storage bag. Combine soy sauce, oil, garlic and red pepper flakes, if desired, in cup; mix well. Pour over shrimp. Seal bag; turn to coat. Marinate at room temperature 15 minutes.

2 Drain shrimp; reserve marinade. Alternately thread shrimp and green onions onto skewers. Brush with reserved marinade; discard any remaining marinade. Grill, covered, 5 minutes per side or until shrimp are pink and opaque. Reserve half of shrimp for Shrimp and Couscous Salad; serve remaining shrimp immediately with rice.

SHRIMP AND COUSCOUS SALAD

makes 6 servings

- 2 cups water
- 2 teaspoons salt, divided
- 1 box (10 ounces) plain uncooked couscous
- 1 medium cucumber, peeled, seeded and diced
- 1 medium poblano chile pepper, seeded and chopped
- 2 avocados, coarsely chopped (¾-inch pieces)

- ½ cup chopped red bell pepper
- 1 can (2¼ ounces) sliced black olives, drained
- ¼ cup chopped fresh cilantro
- ¼ cup extra virgin olive oil
- 1 teaspoon grated lime peel
- 6 tablespoons lime juice (from 3 limes)
- ¼ teaspoon red pepper flakes
- 1 pound shrimp leftover from Garlic Skewered Shrimp (page 77)

1 Bring water and 1 teaspoon salt to a boil in medium saucepan. Place couscous in large bowl. Pour boiling water over couscous. Cover bowl with plastic wrap. Let stand 5 minutes or until water is absorbed. Fluff with fork. Cool to room temperature. (To cool quickly, spread couscous in thin layer on baking sheet or platter.)

2 Add cucumber, poblano pepper, avocados, bell pepper, olives and cilantro to couscous. Whisk oil, lime peel, lime juice, red pepper flakes and remaining 1 teaspoon salt in small bowl. Pour over salad; stir gently to blend. Stir in shrimp. Serve immediately or refrigerate 2 hours before serving. Taste and adjust salt and lime juice before serving.

TIP: To make this recipe without leftovers, use 1 pound frozen cooked shrimp, thawed and patted dry.

MEDITERRANEAN CHICKEN KABOBS OVER COUSCOUS

makes 8 servings with leftovers for Chicken Tzatziki Pitas

- 4 pounds boneless skinless chicken breasts, cut into 1-inch pieces
- 1 small eggplant, peeled and cut into 1-inch pieces
- 1 zucchini, cut crosswise into ½-inch slices
- 2 onions, each cut into 8 wedges
- 16 medium mushrooms
- 16 cherry tomatoes
- 2 cups chicken broth
- 1⅓ cups balsamic vinegar

- 6 tablespoons olive oil
- 3 tablespoons dried mint
- 2 tablespoons dried basil
- 2 tablespoons dried oregano
- 2 teaspoons salt, divided
- 2 cups water
- 1 package (10 ounces) uncooked plain couscous
  Chopped fresh parsley
- 2 teaspoons grated lemon peel

1 Alternately thread half of chicken, eggplant, zucchini, onions, mushrooms and tomatoes onto 16 metal or wooden skewers; place in large glass baking dish. Thread remaining chicken onto additional skewers; place in separate baking dish.

2 Whisk broth, vinegar, oil, mint, basil, oregano and 1 teaspoon salt in medium bowl; pour over kabobs. Cover and marinate in refrigerator 2 hours, turning occasionally. Remove kabobs from marinade; discard marinade.

3 Preheat broiler. Broil kabobs 6 inches from heat 10 to 15 minutes or until chicken is cooked through, turning kabobs halfway through cooking time.

4 Bring water and remaining 1 teaspoon salt to a boil in medium saucepan. Stir in couscous; cover and let stand 5 minutes or until water is absorbed. Fluff with fork. Stir in parsley and lemon peel; taste and add additional parsley, salt and black pepper, if desired. Serve with chicken and veggie kabobs; reserve chicken kabobs to use in sandwiches on page 83.

TIP: These kabobs can be grilled instead of broiled. Spray the grill grid with nonstick cooking spray, then prepare the grill for direct cooking. Grill the kabobs, covered, over medium-hot coals 10 to 15 minutes or until the chicken is cooked through. Turn the kabobs halfway through the cooking time.

CHICKEN TZATZIKI PITAS

makes 4 servings

1 cup plain Greek yogurt
½ cup finely chopped cucumber
1 tablespoon lemon juice
1 tablespoon chopped fresh mint
1 clove garlic, crushed
½ teaspoon salt
 Dash black pepper

Leftover chicken from Mediterranean Chicken Kabobs (page 81), chopped
2 cups chopped romaine lettuce
1 cup chopped tomatoes
¼ cup chopped red onion
¼ cup chopped Greek olives
4 (6-inch) whole wheat pita breads, cut in half

1 Stir together yogurt, cucumber, lemon juice, mint, garlic, salt and pepper in small bowl.

2 Divide chicken, lettuce, tomatoes, onion and olives evenly among pita halves. Serve with sauce.

TACO SALAD SUPREME

makes 4 servings with leftovers for Chili-Topped Baked Potatoes or Chili Mac

CHILI

- 2 pounds ground beef
- 2 medium onions, chopped
- 2 stalks celery, chopped
- 4 medium fresh tomatoes, chopped
- 2 jalapeño peppers, finely chopped
- 1 tablespoon chili powder
- 2 teaspoons salt
- 2 teaspoons ground cumin
- 1 teaspoon black pepper
- 2 cans (15 ounces each) tomato sauce
- 2 cans (about 15 ounces each) kidney beans, rinsed and drained
- 2 cans (about 15 ounces each) pinto beans, rinsed and drained
- 2 cups water

SALAD

- 8 cups chopped romaine lettuce (large pieces)
- 2 cups diced fresh tomatoes
- 48 small round tortilla chips
- 1 cup salsa
- ½ cup sour cream
- 1 cup (4 ounces) shredded Cheddar cheese

1 Combine beef, onions and celery in large saucepan; cook over medium-high heat 6 to 8 minutes or until beef is no longer pink, stirring to break up meat. Drain fat.

2 Add chopped tomatoes, jalapeños, chili powder, salt, cumin and black pepper; cook and stir 1 minute. Stir in tomato sauce, beans and water; bring to a boil. Reduce heat to medium-low; cook about 1 hour or until most of liquid is absorbed.

3 For each salad, combine 2 cups lettuce and ½ cup diced tomatoes in individual bowls. Top with 12 tortilla chips, ¾ cup chili, ¼ cup salsa and 2 tablespoons sour cream. Sprinkle with ¼ cup cheese. Reserve remaining chili for Chili-Topped Baked Potatoes or Chili Mac.

TIP: The chili can be made ahead through step 2. Cool the chili and place it in jars or food storage containers. Reheat it in the microwave or in a saucepan before serving.

CHILI-TOPPED BAKED POTATOES

makes 4 servings

 4 large baking potatoes
 ½ chili recipe leftover from Taco Salad
    Supreme (page 85)

Optional toppings: shredded Cheddar
cheese, sour cream, chopped green
onions and/or diced avocado

1 Preheat oven to 400°F. Poke potatoes all over with fork; place in small baking pan. Bake about 1 hour or until potatoes are fork-tender. Let stand until cool enough to handle. Cut off thin slice from one long side of each potato. Scoop out centers of potatoes, leaving ½-inch shells.

2 Heat chili in medium saucepan over medium heat until hot, stirring occasionally. Spoon chili into potatoes; top with desired toppings.

CHILI MAC

makes 4 servings

½ chili recipe leftover from Taco Salad Supreme (page 85)

½ recipe Classic Macaroni and Cheese (page 53)

1 cup (4 ounces) Mexican shredded cheese blend

1 Place chili in large saucepan; heat over medium heat until hot, stirring occasionally.

2 Stir in macaroni and cheese; cook until heated through, stirring frequently. Scoop into bowls; sprinkle with cheese blend.

SUPER EASY SANDWICHES

chapter four

Sandwiches are the quintessential lunch food but don't underestimate their dinner potential. Everyone loves them, their fillings can be kept in the refrigerator for days and they make excellent quick and easy meals. Plus, they're easy to serve on nights when dinner time is different for everyone, and leftovers make perfect packable lunches.

ALMOND CHICKEN SALAD SANDWICH

makes 4 servings

¼ cup mayonnaise

¼ cup plain Greek yogurt or sour cream

2 tablespoons cider vinegar

1 tablespoon honey

1 teaspoon salt

½ teaspoon black pepper

⅛ teaspoon garlic powder

2 cups chopped cooked chicken

¾ cup halved red grapes

1 large stalk celery, chopped

⅓ cup sliced almonds

Leaf lettuce

1 tomato, thinly sliced

8 slices sesame semolina or country Italian bread

1 Whisk mayonnaise, yogurt, vinegar, honey, salt, pepper and garlic powder in small bowl until well blended.

2 Combine chicken, grapes and celery in medium bowl. Add dressing; toss gently to coat. Cover and refrigerate several hours or overnight. Stir in almonds just before making sandwiches.

3 Place lettuce and tomato slices on 4 bread slices; top with chicken salad and remaining bread slices. Serve immediately.

TIP: To bring for lunch, pack the chicken salad in a food storage container and refrigerate until ready to use. Wrap bread in plastic wrap and store at room temperature.

GRILLED ITALIAN CHICKEN PANINI

makes 6 sandwiches

6 small portobello mushroom caps (about 6 ounces)

½ cup plus 2 tablespoons balsamic vinaigrette dressing

1 loaf (16 ounces) Italian bread, cut into 12 slices

12 slices provolone cheese

1½ cups chopped cooked chicken

1 jar (12 ounces) roasted red peppers, drained

1 Brush mushrooms with 2 tablespoons dressing. Place mushrooms in large nonstick skillet; cook over medium-high heat 5 to 7 minutes or until soft, turning occasionally. Transfer to cutting board; cut diagonally into ½-inch slices.

2 For each sandwich, top 1 bread slice with 1 cheese slice, ¼ cup chicken, mushrooms, roasted red peppers, another cheese slice and another bread slice. Brush outsides of sandwiches with remaining dressing.

3 Preheat grill pan and panini press* at medium heat 5 minutes. Grill sandwiches 4 to 6 minutes or until cheese is melted and bread is golden, turning once during cooking.

*If you don't have a grill pan and panini press, grill sandwiches in a nonstick skillet. Place a clean heavy pan on top of sandwiches to weigh them down while cooking.

TIP: A rotisserie chicken will yield just enough chopped chicken for this recipe.

BLT SUPREME

makes 2 servings

12 to 16 slices thick-cut bacon

1/3 cup mayonnaise

1 1/2 teaspoons minced chipotle pepper in adobo sauce

1 teaspoon lime juice

1 ripe avocado

1/8 teaspoon salt

1/8 teaspoon black pepper

4 leaves romaine lettuce

1/2 baguette, cut into 2 (8-inch) lengths or 2 hoagie rolls, split and toasted

6 to 8 slices tomato

1 Cook bacon in skillet until crisp. Drain on paper towel-lined plate.

2 Meanwhile, combine mayonnaise, chipotle peppers and lime juice in small bowl; mix well. Coarsely mash avocado in another small bowl; stir in salt and black pepper. Cut romaine leaves crosswise into 1/4-inch strips.

3 For each sandwich, spread heaping tablespoon mayonnaise mixture on bottom half of baguette; top with one fourth of lettuce. Arrange 3 to 4 slices bacon over lettuce; spread 2 tablespoons mashed avocado over bacon. Drizzle with heaping tablespoon mayonnaise mixture. Top with 3 to 4 tomato slices, one fourth of lettuce and 3 to 4 slices bacon. Close sandwich with top half of baguette.

TIP: You can cook bacon in the oven instead of a skillet. Preheat the oven to 375°F. Line sheet pan with heavy-duty foil. Arrange bacon on prepared pan, cutting in half to fit, if necessary. Bake 20 to 25 minutes or until bacon is well browned. Carefully remove sheet pan from oven. Immediately remove bacon to paper towel-lined plate.

TOMATO MOZZARELLA SANDWICH

makes 4 servings

BALSAMIC VINAIGRETTE

- 6 tablespoons extra virgin olive oil
- 3 tablespoons balsamic vinegar
- 1 clove garlic, minced
- 1 teaspoon honey
- 1 teaspoon Dijon mustard
- ½ teaspoon dried oregano
- ½ teaspoon salt
- ⅛ teaspoon black pepper

SANDWICHES

- 1 baguette, ends trimmed, cut into 4 equal pieces (4 ounces each) and split
- 1 cup loosely packed baby arugula
- 3 medium tomatoes, sliced ¼ inch thick
- 1 cup roasted red peppers, patted dry and thinly sliced
- 12 slices fresh mozzarella (one 8-ounce package)
- 12 fresh basil leaves

1 For vinaigrette, whisk oil, vinegar, garlic, honey, mustard, oregano, salt and pepper in small bowl until well blended.

2 For each sandwich, drizzle 1 tablespoon vinaigrette over bottom half of bread. Layer with arugula, tomato slices, roasted peppers, cheese slices, additional arugula and basil. Drizzle with 1 tablespoon dressing; replace top half of bread.

SOUTHWEST TURKEY SANDWICH

makes 4 servings

½ cup mayonnaise

1 tablespoon minced chipotle peppers in adobo sauce

1½ teaspoons lime juice

1 round loaf (16 ounces) cheese focaccia or cheese bread (preferably Asiago cheese)

1½ cups mixed greens

12 ounces sliced smoked turkey

½ red onion, thinly sliced

1 Combine mayonnaise, chipotle peppers and lime juice in small bowl; mix well.

2 Cut loaf in half horizontally; spread cut sides of bread with mayonnaise mixture. Top bottom half of loaf with mixed greens, turkey, onion and top half of bread. Cut into wedges.

CUBAN PORK SANDWICH

makes 4 servings

⅓ cup orange juice

3 tablespoons lime juice

1 small onion, finely chopped (½ cup)

3 tablespoons olive oil

6 cloves garlic, minced

2 teaspoons ground cumin

2 teaspoons dried oregano

1 teaspoon salt

1 teaspoon black pepper

2 pounds boneless pork shoulder

4 Cuban sandwich rolls, split*

⅓ cup mayonnaise

⅓ cup yellow mustard

8 ounces sliced Swiss cheese

8 ounces sliced honey ham

8 long thin dill pickle slices

If Cuban rolls are unavailable, substitute a long French or Italian loaf, split in half horizontally and cut into 4 pieces.

1 Combine orange juice, lime juice, onion, oil, garlic, cumin, oregano, salt and pepper in medium bowl; mix well. Place pork in large resealable food storage bag. Pour marinade over pork; seal bag and turn to coat. Marinate in refrigerator at least 2 hours or overnight.

2 Preheat oven to 325°F. Line shallow roasting pan or baking dish with heavy-duty foil. Place pork in prepared pan with half of marinade; discard remaining marinade. Roast about 3 hours or until pork is tender and temperature reaches 160°F. Let stand at least 15 minutes before slicing. (Pork can be prepared in advance and refrigerated.)

3 Slice pork. Spread both cut sides of rolls with mayonnaise, then mustard. Top bottom halves of rolls with half of cheese, ham, pickles, pork, remaining cheese and top halves of rolls.

4 Cook sandwiches in sandwich press, grill pan or hot skillet over medium heat until bread is browned and crisp. (If using grill pan or skillet, use second skillet to press down and compress sandwiches; cook about 5 minutes per side until bread is crisp.)

TIP: About half of the pork is needed for sandwiches; you can freeze the remaining pork for later to use in more sandwiches. Or make the other half into bowls with cooked white rice, drained canned black beans, sliced avocado and salsa verde.

NEW ORLEANS-STYLE MUFFALETTA

makes 4 to 6 servings

¾ cup pitted green olives

½ cup pitted kalamata olives

½ cup giardiniera (Italian-style pickled vegetables), drained

2 tablespoons fresh parsley

2 tablespoons capers

1 clove garlic, minced

2 tablespoons olive oil

1 tablespoon red wine vinegar

1 (8-inch) short round Italian loaf (16 to 22 ounces)

8 ounces thinly sliced ham

8 ounces thinly sliced Genoa salami

6 ounces thinly sliced provolone cheese

1 Combine olives, giardiniera, parsley, capers and garlic in food processor; pulse until coarsely chopped and no large pieces remain. Transfer to small bowl; stir in oil and vinegar until well blended. Cover and refrigerate several hours or overnight to blend flavors.

2 Cut bread in half crosswise. Spread two thirds of olive salad over bottom half of bread; layer with ham, salami and cheese. Spread remaining olive salad over cheese; top with top half of bread, pressing down slightly to compress. Wrap sandwich in plastic wrap; let stand 1 hour to blend flavors.

3 To serve sandwich warm, preheat oven to 350°F. Remove plastic wrap; wrap sandwich loosely in foil. Bake 5 to 10 minutes or just until sandwich is slightly warm and cheese begins to melt. Cut into wedges.

TUNA SALAD SANDWICH

makes 2 servings

1 can (12 ounces) solid white albacore tuna, drained

1 can (5 ounces) chunk white albacore tuna, drained

¼ cup mayonnaise

1 tablespoon pickle relish

2 teaspoons spicy brown mustard

1 teaspoon lemon juice

½ teaspoon salt

¼ teaspoon black pepper

2 pieces focaccia (about 4×3 inches), split and toasted or 4 slices honey wheat bread

Lettuce, tomato and red onion slices

1 Place tuna in medium bowl; flake with fork. Add mayonnaise, relish, mustard, lemon juice, salt and pepper; mix well.

2 Serve tuna salad on focaccia with lettuce, tomato and onion.

CHICKPEA SALAD

makes 2 cups (4 to 6 servings)

1 can (15 ounces) chickpeas, rinsed and drained

1 stalk celery, chopped

1 dill pickle, chopped (about ½ cup)

¼ cup finely chopped red or yellow onion

⅓ cup mayonnaise

1 teaspoon lemon juice

¼ teaspoon salt

Black pepper

Whole grain bread

Lettuce and tomato slices

1 Place chickpeas in medium bowl. Coarsely mash with potato masher, leaving some beans whole.

2 Add celery, pickle and onion; stir to mix. Add mayonnaise and lemon juice; mix well. Taste and add ¼ teaspoon salt or more, if desired. Sprinkle with pepper, if desired; mix well. Serve on bread with lettuce and tomato.

CLASSIC EGG SALAD SANDWICH

makes 4 servings

6 eggs

2 tablespoons mayonnaise*

2 tablespoons sour cream*

½ cup finely chopped celery

1½ tablespoons sweet pickle relish

⅛ to ¼ teaspoon salt

Black pepper

8 slices whole grain bread

Or use ¼ cup mayonnaise instead of half mayonnaise and sour cream.

1 Bring medium saucepan of water to a boil over high heat. Carefully add eggs using slotted spoon. Immediately reduce heat to maintain a gentle boil; cook 12 minutes. Drain and rinse under cold water until cool enough to handle.

2 Coarsely chop eggs; place in medium bowl. Add mayonnaise, sour cream, celery, pickle relish and salt; mix well. Season with pepper.

3 Spread ½ cup egg salad on each of 4 bread slices; top with remaining bread slices.

SHEET PAN &
ONE-POT DINNERS

chapter five

Why use every pan in your kitchen to make dinner when just one will do? When you need a hot cooked meal but don't want to spend all day on it, look no further than a sheet pan or Dutch oven. Prep for a few minutes (either just before cooking or a day or two before) and then let your dinner simmer or roast unattended while you get on with your day.

SHEET PAN CHICKEN AND SAUSAGE SUPPER

makes about 6 servings

⅓ cup olive oil

2 tablespoons balsamic vinegar

1 teaspoon salt

1 teaspoon garlic powder

½ teaspoon black pepper

¼ teaspoon red pepper flakes

3 pounds bone-in chicken thighs and drumsticks

1 pound uncooked sweet Italian sausage (4 to 5 links), cut diagonally into 2-inch pieces

6 to 8 small red onions (about 1½ pounds), each cut into 6 wedges

4 cups broccoli florets

1 Preheat oven to 425°F. Line sheet pan with foil, if desired.

2 Whisk oil, vinegar, salt, garlic powder, black pepper and red pepper flakes in small bowl until well blended. Combine chicken, sausage and onions on prepared sheet pan. Drizzle with oil mixture; toss until well coated. Spread meat and onions in single layer (chicken thighs should be skin side up).

3 Bake 30 minutes. Add broccoli to sheet pan; stir to coat broccoli with pan juices and turn sausage. Bake 30 minutes or until broccoli is beginning to brown and chicken is cooked through (165°F).

SKILLET LASAGNA WITH VEGETABLES

makes 4 servings

8 ounces hot Italian turkey sausage, casings removed

8 ounces ground turkey

2 stalks celery, sliced

⅓ cup chopped onion

2 cups marinara sauce

1⅓ cups water

4 ounces uncooked bowtie (farfalle) pasta

1 medium zucchini, halved lengthwise, then cut crosswise into ½-inch slices (2 cups)

¾ cup chopped green or yellow bell pepper

½ cup (2 ounces) shredded mozzarella cheese

½ cup ricotta cheese

2 tablespoons finely grated Parmesan cheese

1 Heat large skillet over medium-high heat. Add sausage, ground turkey, celery and onion; cook and stir 6 to 8 minutes or until turkey is no longer pink. Stir in marinara sauce and water; bring to a boil. Stir in pasta. Reduce heat to medium-low; cover and simmer 12 minutes.

2 Stir in zucchini and bell pepper; cover and simmer 2 minutes. Uncover and simmer 4 to 6 minutes or until vegetables are crisp-tender.

3 Sprinkle with mozzarella. Combine ricotta and Parmesan in small bowl; stir to blend. Drop by rounded teaspoonfuls on top of mixture in skillet. Remove from heat; cover and let stand 10 minutes.

CHICKEN SCARPIELLO

makes 6 servings

3 tablespoons extra virgin olive oil, divided

1 pound spicy Italian sausage, cut into 1-inch pieces

1 whole chicken (about 3 pounds), cut into 10 pieces*

1 teaspoon salt, divided

1 large onion, chopped

2 red, yellow or orange bell peppers, cut into ¼-inch strips

3 cloves garlic, minced

½ cup white wine

½ cup chicken broth

½ cup coarsely chopped seeded hot cherry peppers

½ cup liquid from cherry pepper jar

1 teaspoon dried oregano
   Additional salt and black pepper

¼ cup chopped fresh Italian parsley

*Or purchase 2 bone-in chicken leg quarters and 2 chicken breasts; separate drumsticks and thighs and cut breasts in half.

1 Heat 1 tablespoon oil in large skillet over medium-high heat. Add sausage; cook about 10 minutes or until well browned on all sides, stirring occasionally. Remove sausage from skillet; set aside.

2 Heat 1 tablespoon oil in same skillet. Sprinkle chicken with ½ teaspoon salt; arrange skin side down in single layer in skillet (cook in batches, if necessary). Cook about 6 minutes per side or until browned. Remove chicken from skillet; set aside. Drain oil from skillet.

3 Heat remaining 1 tablespoon oil in skillet. Add onion and ½ teaspoon salt; cook and stir 2 minutes or until onion is softened, scraping up browned bits from bottom of skillet. Add bell peppers and garlic; cook and stir 5 minutes. Stir in wine; cook until liquid is reduced by half. Stir in broth, cherry peppers, cherry pepper liquid and oregano. Season with additional salt and black pepper; bring to a simmer.

4 Return sausage and chicken along with any accumulated juices to skillet. Partially cover skillet; simmer 10 minutes. Uncover; simmer 15 minutes or until chicken is cooked through (165°F). Sprinkle with parsley.

TIP: If too much liquid remains in the skillet when the chicken is cooked through, remove the chicken and sausage and continue simmering the sauce to reduce it slightly.

PASTA FAGIOLI

makes 8 servings (13 cups)

2 tablespoons olive oil, divided	2 teaspoons sugar
1 pound ground beef	1½ teaspoons dried basil
1 cup chopped onion	1¼ teaspoons salt
1 cup diced carrots (about 2 medium)	1 teaspoon dried oregano
1 cup diced celery (about 2 stalks)	¾ teaspoon dried thyme
3 cloves garlic, minced	2 cups uncooked ditalini pasta
4 cups beef broth	1 can (15 ounces) dark red kidney beans, rinsed and drained
1 can (28 ounces) diced tomatoes	
1 can (15 ounces) tomato sauce	1 can (15 ounces) cannellini beans, rinsed and drained
1 tablespoon cider vinegar	Grated Romano cheese

1 Heat 1 tablespoon oil in large saucepan or Dutch oven over medium-high heat. Add beef; cook 5 minutes or until browned, stirring to break up meat. Transfer to medium bowl. Drain fat from saucepan.

2 Heat remaining 1 tablespoon oil in same saucepan over medium-high heat. Add onion, carrots and celery; cook and stir 5 minutes or until vegetables are tender. Add garlic; cook and stir 1 minute. Add cooked beef, broth, tomatoes, tomato sauce, vinegar, sugar, basil, salt, oregano and thyme; bring to a boil. Reduce heat to medium-low; cover and simmer 30 minutes.

3 Add pasta, kidney beans and cannellini beans; cook over medium heat 10 minutes or until pasta is tender, stirring frequently. Ladle into bowls; top with cheese.

TIP: To make ahead, cook soup and transfer it to jars or large food storage containers. Reheat in a saucepan over medium heat until hot.

ROAST CHICKEN AND POTATOES CATALAN

makes 4 servings

- 2 tablespoons olive oil
- 2 tablespoons lemon juice
- 1 teaspoon dried thyme
- ½ teaspoon salt
- ¼ teaspoon ground red pepper
- ¼ teaspoon ground saffron or ½ teaspoon crushed saffron threads or turmeric

- 2 large baking potatoes (about 1½ pounds), cut into 1½-inch pieces
- 4 skinless bone-in chicken breasts (about 2 pounds)
- 1 cup sliced red bell pepper
- 1 cup frozen peas, thawed
  Lemon wedges (optional)

1 Preheat oven to 400°F. Spray large shallow roasting pan or 15×10-inch jelly-roll pan with nonstick cooking spray.

2 Combine oil, lemon juice, thyme, salt, ground red pepper and saffron in large bowl; mix well. Add potatoes; toss to coat.

3 Arrange potatoes in single layer around edges of pan. Place chicken in center of pan; brush both sides of chicken with remaining oil mixture in bowl.

4 Bake 20 minutes. Turn potatoes; baste chicken with pan juices. Add bell pepper; continue baking 20 minutes or until chicken is no longer pink in center, juices run clear and potatoes are browned. Stir peas into potato mixture; bake 5 minutes or until heated through. Garnish with lemon wedges.

CHICKPEA TIKKA MASALA

makes 4 servings

1 tablespoon olive oil

1 onion, chopped

3 cloves garlic, minced

1 tablespoon minced fresh ginger or ginger paste

1 tablespoon garam masala

1 teaspoon ground cumin

1 teaspoon ground coriander

1 teaspoon salt

¼ teaspoon ground red pepper

2 cans (15 ounces each) chickpeas, drained

1 can (28 ounces) crushed tomatoes

1 can (about 13 ounces) coconut milk

1 package (about 12 ounces) firm silken tofu, drained and cut into 1-inch cubes

Hot cooked brown basmati rice

Chopped fresh cilantro

1 Heat oil in large saucepan over medium-high heat. Add onion; cook and stir 5 minutes or until translucent. Add garlic, ginger, garam masala, cumin, coriander, salt and red pepper; cook and stir 1 minute.

2 Stir in chickpeas, tomatoes and coconut milk; simmer 30 minutes or until thickened and chickpeas have softened slightly. Add tofu; stir gently. Cook 7 to 10 minutes or until tofu is heated through. Serve over rice; garnish with cilantro.

TIP: Make ahead through adding the tofu. Cool and transfer to food storage containers or jars. Gently reheat in medium saucepan over medium heat until heated through. Add the tofu; cook 7 to 10 minutes or until heated through.

CAULIFLOWER, SAUSAGE AND GOUDA SHEET PAN

makes 6 servings

1 package (16 ounces) white mushrooms, stemmed and halved

3 tablespoons olive oil, divided

1 teaspoon salt, divided

1 head cauliflower, separated into florets and thinly sliced

1/4 teaspoon chipotle chili powder

1 package (about 13 ounces) smoked sausage, cut into 1/4-inch slices

2 tablespoons peach or apricot preserves

1 tablespoon Dijon mustard

1/2 red onion, thinly sliced

6 ounces Gouda cheese, cubed

1 Preheat oven to 400°F.

2 Place mushrooms in medium bowl. Drizzle with 1 tablespoon oil and sprinkle with 1/2 teaspoon salt; toss to coat. Spread on sheet pan.

3 Place cauliflower, remaining 2 tablespoons oil, 1/2 teaspoon salt and chipotle chili powder in same bowl; toss to coat. Spread on sheet pan with mushrooms.

4 Combine sausage, preserves and mustard in same bowl; stir until well coated. Arrange sausage over vegetables; top with onion.

5 Roast 30 minutes. Remove from oven; place cheese cubes on top of cauliflower. Bake 5 minutes or until cheese is melted and cauliflower is tender.

PASTA E CECI

makes 4 servings

4 tablespoons olive oil, divided

1 onion, chopped

1 carrot, chopped

1 clove garlic, minced

1 fresh rosemary sprig

1 teaspoon salt

1 can (28 ounces) whole tomatoes, drained and crushed

2 cups vegetable broth or water

1 can (15 ounces) chickpeas, undrained

1 bay leaf

⅛ teaspoon red pepper flakes

1 cup uncooked orecchiette

Black pepper

Chopped fresh parsley or basil

1 Heat 3 tablespoons oil in large saucepan over medium-high heat. Add onion and carrot; cook 10 minutes or until vegetables are softened, stirring occasionally.

2 Add garlic, rosemary and 1 teaspoon salt; cook and stir 1 minute. Stir in tomatoes, broth, chickpeas with liquid, bay leaf and red pepper flakes. Remove 1 cup mixture to food processor or blender; process until smooth. Stir back into saucepan; bring to a boil.

3 Stir in pasta. Reduce heat to medium; cook 12 to 15 minutes or until pasta is tender and mixture is creamy. Remove and discard bay leaf and rosemary sprig. Taste and season with additional salt and black pepper, if desired. Divide among bowls; garnish with parsley and drizzle with remaining 1 tablespoon oil.

NOTE: To crush the tomatoes, take them out of the can one at a time and crush them between your fingers over the saucepan. Or coarsely chop them with a knife.

HONEY LEMON GARLIC CHICKEN

makes 4 servings

2 lemons, divided

2 tablespoons butter, melted

2 tablespoons honey

3 cloves garlic, chopped

2 sprigs fresh rosemary, leaves removed from stems

1 teaspoon coarse salt

½ teaspoon black pepper

3 pounds chicken (4 bone-in skin-on chicken thighs and 4 drumsticks)

1¼ pounds unpeeled small potatoes, cut into halves or quarters

1 Preheat oven to 375°F. Grate peel and squeeze juice from 1 lemon. Cut remaining lemon into slices.

2 Combine lemon peel, lemon juice, butter, honey, garlic, rosemary leaves, salt and pepper in small bowl; mix well. Combine chicken, potatoes and lemon slices in large bowl. Pour butter mixture over chicken, potatoes and lemon slices; toss to coat. Arrange in single layer on large rimmed baking sheet or in shallow roasting pan.

3 Bake about 1 hour or until potatoes are tender and chicken is cooked through (165°F). Cover loosely with foil if chicken skin is becoming too dark.

PACKABLE SALADS

chapter six

Some of these salads may look daunting with long ingredient lists and various components, but you get a lot of payoff for your efforts. Salads pack really well for lunches and will save you time and money by not going out to a restaurant. And all of the components can be made or assembled ahead of time, and at different times. Salad dressings can be stored for at least a week in the refrigerator and toppings like toasted or caramelized nuts will be fine at room temperature for awhile. And the non-lettuce salads like Texas Caviar and Sesame Noodles benefit from time spent in the fridge as their flavors blend and get even better.

STRAWBERRY CHICKEN SALAD

makes 4 servings

GLAZED WALNUTS

- 2 tablespoons butter
- 6 tablespoons sugar
- 1 tablespoon honey
- ½ teaspoon salt
- ⅛ teaspoon ground red pepper
- 1 cup walnuts

DRESSING

- 1 cup fresh strawberries, hulled
- ½ cup vegetable oil
- 6 tablespoons white wine vinegar
- 3 tablespoons sugar
- 3 tablespoons honey
- 2 tablespoons balsamic vinegar
- 2 teaspoons Dijon mustard
- ½ teaspoon dried oregano
- ¼ teaspoon salt

SALAD

- 4 cups chopped romaine lettuce
- 4 cups coarsely chopped fresh spinach
- 2 cups cooked chicken slices (about half of a rotisserie chicken)
- 1 cup sliced fresh strawberries
- ½ cup crumbled feta cheese

1 For walnuts, preheat oven to 350°F. Line baking sheet with foil; spray with nonstick cooking spray.

2 Melt butter in medium skillet over medium-high heat. Stir in 6 tablespoons sugar, 1 tablespoon honey, ½ teaspoon salt and red pepper until well blended. Add walnuts; cook 3 minutes or until nuts are glazed and begin to brown, stirring occasionally. Spread in single layer on prepared baking sheet. Bake 7 minutes or until nuts are lightly browned and fragrant. Cool completely on baking sheet. Break into individual nuts.

3 For dressing, combine whole strawberries, oil, white wine vinegar, 3 tablespoons sugar, 3 tablespoons honey, balsamic vinegar, mustard, oregano and ¼ teaspoon salt in blender or food processor; blend 30 seconds or until smooth.

4 For each salad, combine 1 cup lettuce and 1 cup spinach in serving bowl or food storage container; top with chicken. Store in the refrigerator until ready to eat. Pack ¼ cup sliced strawberries, ¼ cup glazed walnuts and 2 tablespoons cheese separately for each serving. Mix together just before serving and drizzle with 2 tablespoons dressing.

TIP: Nuts and dressing can be made a few days ahead of time. Store dressing in a jar (or several small jars) in the refrigerator. Store nuts in food storage bags at room temperature.

SESAME NOODLES

makes 6 servings

1 package (16 ounces) uncooked spaghetti

6 tablespoons soy sauce

5 tablespoons dark sesame oil

3 tablespoons sugar

3 tablespoons rice vinegar

2 tablespoons vegetable oil

3 cloves garlic, minced

1 teaspoon grated fresh ginger or ginger paste

½ teaspoon sriracha sauce

2 green onions, sliced

1 red bell pepper

1 cucumber

1 carrot

Sesame seeds (optional)

1 Cook spaghetti according to package directions until al dente in large saucepan of boiling salted water. Drain, reserving 1 tablespoon pasta cooking water.

2 Whisk soy sauce, sesame oil, sugar, vinegar, vegetable oil, garlic, ginger, sriracha and reserved pasta water in large bowl. Stir in noodles and green onions. Let stand at least 30 minutes until noodles have cooled to room temperature and most of sauce is absorbed, stirring occasionally.

3 Meanwhile, cut bell pepper into thin strips. Peel cucumber and carrot and shred with julienne peeler into long strands, or cut into thin strips. Stir into noodles. Pack individual servings in food storage containers; refrigerate until ready to serve. Top with sesame seeds just before serving, if desired.

TEXAS CAVIAR

makes 8 to 10 servings (9 cups)

1 tablespoon vegetable oil

1 cup fresh corn (from 2 to 3 ears)

3 cups cooked black-eyed peas (see Note)

1 can (15 ounces) black beans

1 cup halved grape tomatoes

1 bell pepper (red, orange, yellow or green), finely chopped

½ cup finely chopped red onion

1 jalapeño pepper, seeded and minced

2 green onions, minced

¼ cup chopped fresh cilantro

2 tablespoons red wine vinegar

1 tablespoon plus 1 teaspoon lime juice, divided

1 teaspoon salt

1 teaspoon sugar

½ teaspoon ground cumin

½ teaspoon dried oregano

2 cloves garlic, minced

¼ cup olive oil

Tortilla chips, corn chips or shredded iceberg lettuce

1 Heat vegetable oil in large skillet over high heat. Add corn; cook and stir about 3 minutes or until corn is beginning to brown in spots. Place in large bowl. Add beans, tomatoes, bell pepper, onion, jalapeño, green onions and cilantro.

2 Combine vinegar, 1 tablespoon lime juice, salt, sugar, cumin, oregano and garlic in small bowl. Whisk in olive oil in thin steady stream until well blended. Pour over vegetables; stir to coat. Pack in food storage containers and refrigerate until ready to serve. If desired, pack tortilla chips or lettuce separately and serve with salad.

NOTE: For black-eyed peas, use 2 (15-ounce) cans, rinsed and drained, if you can find them, or cook the beans from dried. Soak 8 ounces of dried beans in salted water at least 4 hours or overnight. Drain beans and place in large saucepan. Cover with water and bring to a boil over high heat. Reduce heat; simmer 45 minutes to 1 hour or until beans are tender. Drain and let cool before using.

MEDITERREAN PASTA SALAD IN A JAR

makes 6 (2-cup) servings

PASTA SALAD

- 6 cups cooked regular or multigrain rotini pasta
- 1½ cups diced cucumber
- 1 cup diced tomatoes (about 2 medium)
- 1 cup diced green bell pepper (about 1 medium)
- 1 package (4 ounces) crumbled feta cheese
- 12 medium pitted black olives, sliced
- ¼ cup chopped fresh dill

DRESSING

- ¼ cup olive oil
- ¼ cup lemon juice
- ¼ teaspoon salt
- ¼ teaspoon dried oregano
- ⅛ teaspoon black pepper

1 For pasta salad, combine pasta, cucumber, tomatoes, bell pepper, cheese, olives and dill in large bowl; toss to blend.

2 For dressing, combine oil, lemon juice, salt, oregano and black pepper in small bowl; stir to blend. Pour over pasta; toss well to coat.

3 Spoon about 2 cups pasta salad into each of six (1-pint) resealable jars. Seal jars. Refrigerate until ready to serve.

ITALIAN BREAD SALAD

makes 4 (2-cup) servings

4 slices Italian bread, cut into ½-inch cubes (about 4 cups)

½ cup buttermilk

1 clove garlic, minced

1 tablespoon minced fresh dill or 1 teaspoon dried dill weed

1½ teaspoons onion powder

¼ teaspoon salt, plus additional as needed

¼ teaspoon black pepper

½ cup cherry tomatoes, quartered

1 cucumber, peeled, cut in half lengthwise, seeded and thinly sliced

1 stalk celery, thinly sliced

2 tablespoons minced fresh basil

1 Preheat oven to 400°F. Spread bread cubes on baking sheet. Bake 5 to 7 minutes or until lightly toasted and dry, stirring occasionally. Cool completely on baking sheet.

2 Whisk buttermilk, garlic, dill, onion powder, ¼ teaspoon salt and pepper in small bowl until well blended. Let stand 15 minutes to allow flavors to blend.

3 Spoon equal amounts bread cubes into bottom of four (1-pint) resealable jars. Layer tomatoes, cucumber, celery and basil over bread. Sprinkle with additional salt, if desired.

4 Stir dressing; pour equal amounts over salads. Seal jars; shake to distribute dressing. Refrigerate until ready to serve.

COBB SALAD TO GO

makes 4 servings

½ cup blue cheese salad dressing

1 ripe avocado, diced

1 tomato, chopped

6 ounces cooked chicken breast, cut into 1-inch pieces

4 slices bacon, crisp-cooked and crumbled

2 hard-cooked eggs, mashed

1 large carrot, shredded

½ cup blue cheese, crumbled

1 package (10 ounces) torn mixed salad greens

1 Place 2 tablespoons salad dressing into bottom of four (1-quart) jars. Layer remaining ingredients on top, ending with salad greens. Seal jars.

2 Refrigerate until ready to serve.

CHOPPED SALAD

makes 4 (1-quart) servings

2 tablespoons fresh lemon juice

2 tablespoons fresh lime juice

1 tablespoon creamy peanut butter

1 tablespoon sugar

1 teaspoon sesame seeds

½ teaspoon minced garlic

¼ teaspoon black pepper

1 cup chopped cooked turkey, chicken or ham

2 cups chopped romaine lettuce

3 cups baby spinach, chopped

½ head bok choy, chopped

½ cup baby carrots, chopped

½ cup sugar snap peas, chopped

1 small tomato, chopped

1 Combine lemon juice, lime juice, peanut butter, sugar, sesame seeds, garlic and pepper in small jar with tight-fitting lid. Shake until well blended. Pour evenly into four (½-cup) resealable jars.

2 Layer turkey, romaine, spinach, bok choy, carrots, snap peas and tomato in four (1-quart) jars. Seal with lid. Refrigerate until ready to serve. Serve with dressing.

TACO SALAD

makes 4 (1-quart) jars

DRESSING

- ¼ cup mayonnaise
- ¼ cup plain yogurt or sour cream
- 1 tablespoon lime juice
- ½ teaspoon chipotle chili powder
- 1 clove garlic, minced
- ¼ cup crumbled cotija cheese
- ¼ cup chopped fresh cilantro

SALAD

- 1 tablespoon vegetable oil
- 1 package (16 ounces) frozen corn
- ¼ teaspoon salt
- 1 large avocado, diced
- 1 teaspoon lime juice
- 1 can (about 15 ounces) black beans, rinsed and drained
- 2 medium tomatoes, seeded and diced (1 cup)
- ½ cup finely chopped red onion
  Packaged tortilla strips or corn chips
  Chopped fresh lettuce or spinach

1 For dressing, whisk mayonnaise, yogurt, 1 tablespoon lime juice, chili powder and garlic in small bowl. Stir in cheese and cilantro.

2 For salad, heat oil in saucepan over high heat. Add corn; cook 7 to 10 minutes or until lightly browned, stirring occasionally. Stir in salt. Transfer to medium bowl; cool to room temperature. Combine avocado and 1 teaspoon lime juice in small bowl; toss to coat.

3 For each 1-quart jar, layer 2½ tablespoons dressing, ½ cup corn, scant ½ cup black beans, ¼ cup tomatoes, 2 tablespoons onion and about ¼ cup avocado. Top with tortilla strips and lettuce. Seal jars. Refrigerate until ready to serve.

NOTE: To eat, dump the contents of the jar into a large bowl and scrape the dressing on top. Stir gently to mix.

GREEN GODDESS COBB SALAD

makes 4 servings

PICKLED ONIONS

1 cup thinly sliced red onion
½ cup white wine vinegar
¼ cup water
2 teaspoons sugar
1 teaspoon salt

DRESSING

1 cup mayonnaise
1 cup fresh Italian parsley leaves
1 cup baby arugula
¼ cup extra virgin olive oil
3 tablespoons lemon juice
3 tablespoons minced fresh chives
2 tablespoons fresh tarragon leaves

1 clove garlic, minced
1 teaspoon Dijon mustard
½ teaspoon salt
⅛ teaspoon black pepper

SALAD

4 eggs
4 cups Italian salad blend (romaine and radicchio)
2 cups chopped stemmed kale
2 cups baby arugula
2 avocados, sliced and halved
2 tomatoes, cut into wedges
2 cups cooked chicken strips
1 cup chopped crisp-cooked bacon

1 For pickled onions, combine onion, vinegar, ¼ cup water, sugar and 1 teaspoon salt in large glass jar. Seal jar; shake well. Refrigerate at least 1 hour or up to 1 week.

2 For dressing, combine mayonnaise, parsley, 1 cup arugula, oil, lemon juice, chives, tarragon, garlic, mustard, ½ teaspoon salt and pepper in blender or food processor; blend until smooth, stopping to scrape down side once or twice. Transfer to jar; refrigerate until ready to use. Just before serving, thin dressing with 1 to 2 tablespoons water, if necessary, to reach desired consistency.

3 Fill medium saucepan with water; bring to a boil over high heat. Carefully lower eggs into water. Reduce heat to medium; boil gently 12 minutes. Drain eggs; add cold water and ice cubes to saucepan to cool eggs. When eggs are cool enough to handle, peel and cut in half lengthwise.

4 For each salad, combine 1 cup salad blend, ½ cup kale, ½ cup arugula and ¼ cup pickled onions in food storage container or jar. Top each salad with avocados, tomatoes, chicken, bacon and two egg halves. Pack dressing in small jars; pour over salad just before serving.

CABBAGE SALAD WITH CHICKEN & QUINOA

makes 4 servings

⅔ cup uncooked quinoa

1⅔ cups water

¾ teaspoon salt, divided

1 cup shredded green cabbage*

1 cup shredded red cabbage*

½ cup shredded carrot*

½ cup chopped red onion

½ cup sliced green onions

1 jalapeño, seeded and minced (optional)

¼ cup crushed pineapple

3 tablespoons fresh lime juice

2 tablespoons canola oil

1 tablespoon sugar

2 teaspoons minced fresh ginger

1 package (16 to 20 ounces) cooked chicken strips

Or substitute 1 package (9 ounces) broccoli slaw mix for the green cabbage, red cabbage and carrot.

1 Rinse quinoa under cold water in fine-mesh strainer. Bring 1⅔ cups water, quinoa and ¼ teaspoon salt to a boil in small saucepan. Reduce heat to low; cover and simmer 10 to 15 minutes or until quinoa is tender and water is absorbed. Cool slightly.

2 Meanwhile, combine slaw mix, onion, green onions and jalapeno, if desired, in medium bowl.

3 Whisk pineapple, lime juice, oil, sugar, ginger and ½ teaspoon salt in small bowl until well blended. Stir dressing into cabbage mixture. Pack cabbage salad and quinoa in food storage containers; top with chicken.

FATTOUSH SALAD

makes 4 to 6 servings

2 pita breads

⅓ cup plus 3 tablespoons olive oil, divided

Salt and black pepper

2 cups chopped romaine or green leaf lettuce

1 seedless cucumber, quartered lengthwise and sliced

2 tomatoes, diced

4 green onions, thinly sliced

3 radishes, thinly sliced

¼ cup finely chopped fresh parsley

1 tablespoon finely chopped fresh mint

2 tablespoons pomegranate molasses

2 cloves garlic, minced

2 tablespoons red wine vinegar

1 tablespoon lemon juice

1 Preheat oven to 400°F. Cut pita bread into 1-inch cubes. Toss with 3 tablespoons oil and ½ teaspoon salt in large bowl. Spread on large baking sheet. Bake 10 minutes or until pita cubes are browned and crisp. Cool completely on baking sheet.

2 Combine lettuce, cucumber, tomatoes, green onions, radishes, parsley and mint in large bowl. Add pita cubes.

3 For dressing, combine remaining ⅓ cup oil, pomegranate molasses, garlic, vinegar and lemon juice in small bowl. Season with ½ teaspoon salt and pepper; whisk until well blended. Taste and adjust seasoning. Pour over salad; toss until well blended and ingredients are coated.

TIP: This is a great salad to make if you have leftover pita and vegetables. To keep pita cubes crisp, pack the salad in a jar or food storage container and place pita cubes on top. Or wrap croutons in plastic wrap and place on top of salad.

GRAB-AND-GO BREAKFASTS

chapter seven

All these recipes are easy to prepare the night before and bake in the morning. Or make two on Saturday night, bake them on Sunday morning and pack up the remaining casserole for breakfasts throughout the week.

BAKED PUMPKIN OATMEAL

makes 6 servings

2 cups old-fashioned oats

2 cups milk

1 cup canned pumpkin

2 eggs

⅓ cup packed brown sugar

1 teaspoon vanilla

½ cup dried cranberries, plus additional for topping

1 teaspoon pumpkin pie spice

½ teaspoon salt

½ teaspoon baking powder

Maple syrup

Chopped pecans (optional)

1 Preheat oven to 350°F.

2 Spread oats in ungreased 8-inch square baking dish. Bake 10 minutes or until fragrant and lightly browned, stirring occasionally. Pour into medium bowl; let cool slightly.

3 Spray same baking dish with nonstick cooking spray. Whisk milk, pumpkin, eggs, brown sugar and vanilla in large bowl until well blended. Add ½ cup cranberries, pumpkin pie spice, salt and baking powder to oats; mix well. Add oat mixture to pumpkin mixture; stir until well blended. Pour into prepared baking dish.

4 Bake 45 minutes or until set and knife inserted into center comes out almost clean. Serve warm with maple syrup, additional cranberries and pecans, if desired. Or cool completely and divide into 6 portions; place in food storage containers. Heat individual servings in microwave until hot. Top with syrup, pecans and cranberries.

BLUEBERRY-ORANGE FRENCH TOAST CASSEROLE

makes 6 servings

½ cup sugar

½ cup milk

6 eggs

1 tablespoon grated orange peel

½ teaspoon vanilla

¼ teaspoon salt

6 slices whole wheat bread, cut into 1-inch pieces

1 cup fresh blueberries

1 Preheat oven to 350°F. Spray 8-inch square baking dish with nonstick cooking spray.

2 Whisk sugar and milk in medium bowl until dissolved. Whisk in eggs, orange peel, vanilla and salt. Add bread and blueberries; stir to coat. Pour into prepared dish. Let stand at least 5 minutes or cover and refrigerate overnight.

3 Bake 40 to 45 minutes or until bread is browned and center is almost set. Let stand 5 minutes before serving. Or cool completely and divide into 6 portions; place in food storage containers. Heat individual servings in microwave until hot.

ROASTED PEPPER AND SOURDOUGH BRUNCH CASSEROLE

makes 8 servings

3 cups sourdough bread cubes

1 jar (12 ounces) roasted red pepper strips, drained

1 cup (4 ounces) shredded sharp Cheddar cheese

1 cup (4 ounces) shredded Monterey Jack cheese

1 cup cottage cheese

6 eggs

1 cup milk

¼ cup chopped fresh cilantro

½ teaspoon salt

¼ teaspoon black pepper

1 Spray 11×7-inch baking dish with nonstick cooking spray. Place bread cubes in prepared baking dish. Arrange roasted peppers evenly over bread cubes; sprinkle with Cheddar and Monterey Jack cheeses.

2 Place cottage cheese in food processor or blender; process until smooth. Add eggs and milk; process just until blended. Pour over ingredients in baking dish. Sprinkle with cilantro, salt and black pepper. Cover; refrigerate 4 hours or overnight.

3 Preheat oven to 375°F. Bake, uncovered, 40 minutes or until center is set and top is golden brown. Let stand 5 minutes before serving. Or cool completely and divide into 8 portions; place in food storage containers. Heat individual servings in microwave until hot.

HAM AND CHEESE BREAD PUDDING

makes 8 servings

1 small loaf (8 ounces) sourdough, country French or Italian bread, sliced

3 tablespoons butter, softened

8 ounces ham or smoked ham, cubed

1 cup (4 ounces) shredded Cheddar cheese

3 eggs

2 cups milk

1 teaspoon ground mustard

½ teaspoon salt

⅛ teaspoon white pepper

1 Spray 11×7-inch baking dish with nonstick cooking spray. Spread one side of each bread slice with butter. Cut into 1-inch cubes; place on bottom of prepared dish. Top with ham; sprinkle with cheese.

2 Beat eggs in medium bowl. Whisk in milk, mustard, salt and pepper until blended. Pour egg mixture evenly over bread mixture; cover and refrigerate at least 6 hours or overnight.

3 Preheat oven to 350°F. Bake, uncovered, 45 to 50 minutes or until puffed and golden brown and knife inserted into center comes out clean. Serve immediately. Or cool completely and divide into 8 portions; place in food storage containers. Heat individual servings in microwave until hot.

POTATO, SAUSAGE AND PEPPER BREAKFAST BAKE

makes 4 to 6 servings

1 pound mild bulk pork sausage

3 cups frozen hash brown potatoes, thawed

1 large green bell pepper, diced, or 1 cup frozen thawed diced green bell pepper

1 can (11 ounces) nacho cheese soup, divided

¼ cup milk

1 cup (4 ounces) shredded Cheddar cheese

1 Preheat oven to 350°F. Spray 11×7-inch baking dish with nonstick cooking spray.

2 Brown sausage in large skillet over medium-high heat 6 to 8 minutes, stirring to break up meat. Drain fat. Combine potatoes, bell pepper and two thirds of soup in medium bowl. Pour mixture into prepared baking dish. Layer sausage over potato mixture. Stir remaining soup and milk in small bowl. Spoon over sausage. Sprinkle with cheese.

3 Bake 20 minutes or until cheese is melted and sauce is bubbly. Serve immediately. Or cool completely and divide into 6 portions; place in food storage containers. Heat individual servings in microwave until hot.

NOTE: For a vegetarian casserole substitute meatless soy crumbles for the sausage.

PANCAKE BREAKFAST CASSEROLE

makes 6 to 8 servings

6 eggs
1½ cups half-and-half
3 tablespoons sugar
1 teaspoon ground cinnamon, plus additional for garnish

1 teaspoon vanilla
15 frozen buttermilk pancakes (4-inch diameter), 5 whole and 10 cut in half
Maple syrup

1 Spray 3-quart soufflé dish with nonstick cooking spray. Beat eggs, half-and-half, sugar, 1 teaspoon cinnamon and vanilla in medium bowl until well blended.

2 Arrange 5 whole pancakes standing up around side of prepared dish. Stack pancake halves in soufflé dish, making layers as even as possible. Pour egg mixture over pancakes; press pancakes gently into liquid. Cover with foil; refrigerate overnight.

3 Remove soufflé dish from refrigerator at least 30 minutes before baking. Preheat oven to 350°F.

4 Bake, covered, 55 minutes or until all liquid is absorbed. Let stand 5 minutes before serving. Sprinkle with additional cinnamon, if desired. Cut into wedges; serve warm with maple syrup. Or cool completely and divide into 6 portions; place in food storage containers. Heat individual servings in microwave until hot.

READY-TO-EAT SWEETS

chapter eight

Many desserts can be considered "make ahead"—cookies, cake,
ice cream, pies, just to name a few. But the focus of this chapter
is relatively easy and nearly no-bake recipes that will keep for
awhile and satisfy a small craving for something sweet. A notable
exception is the chocolate cake milkshake but it's in the spirit of
meal prep. Make an easy layer cake from a mix (with a secret
ingredient!), and you've got the base for a decadent milkshake,
cake bonbons and just chocolate cake that you can serve or
freeze to make more milkshakes later.

SPRINKLE CAKE AND ICE CREAM JARS

makes 20 (1-pint) jars

CAKE

- 2 cups all-purpose flour
- 4 teaspoons baking powder
- ½ teaspoon salt
- 1½ cups granulated sugar
- ½ cup (1 stick) butter, softened
- 1 cup milk
- 1 teaspoon vanilla
- 3 eggs
- ½ cup rainbow sprinkles

FROSTING

- ½ cup (1 stick) butter, softened
- 3 cups powdered sugar
- 3 tablespoons whipping cream
- ½ teaspoon vanilla

GARNISHES

- Ice cream
- Chocolate ice cream topping
- Additional sprinkles

1 Preheat oven to 350°F. Spray jelly-roll pan with nonstick cooking spray; line with parchment paper.

2 Sift flour, baking powder and salt in large bowl. Stir in granulated sugar. Add ½ cup butter, milk and 1 teaspoon vanilla; beat with electric mixer on low speed 30 seconds. Beat on medium speed 2 minutes. Add eggs; beat 2 minutes. Fold in ½ cup sprinkles. Pour into prepared pan.

3 Bake 18 to 20 minutes or until toothpick inserted into center comes out clean. Cool completely in pan on wire rack.

4 For frosting, beat ½ cup butter in large bowl on medium speed 30 seconds or until creamy. Gradually add powdered sugar alternately with whipping cream; add ½ teaspoon vanilla. Beat on medium-high speed until light and fluffy.

5 Cut cake in half crosswise. Spread half of frosting over one cake half; top with remaining cake. Spread remaining frosting over top of cake; sprinkle with additional sprinkles.

6 Cut cake into circles or squares that will fit into jars; place one cake circle into each jar. Top with scoop of ice cream, chocolate ice cream topping and additional sprinkles, as desired. Freeze until ready to serve.

LEFTOVER CANDY BARK

makes about 3 pounds

3 cups chopped leftover chocolate candy

2 packages (12 ounces each) white chocolate chips

1 package (10 ounces) peanut butter chips

1 Line 13×9-inch baking pan with parchment paper. Spread candy in prepared baking pan and freeze at least 1 hour.

2 Melt white chocolate and peanut butter chips in large microwavable bowl on HIGH at 45-second intervals, stirring after each interval, until melted and smooth, about 5 minutes total. Towards the end, check every 20 to 30 seconds. Stir in 2½ cups candy and spread evenly in same parchment-lined baking pan; sprinkle with remaining ½ cup candy. Refrigerate about 1 hour or until firm. Break into pieces.

TIP: For thinner bark, use a sheet pan instead of a 13×9-inch baking pan.

CAKE BONBONS

makes 32 to 36 bonbons

4 cups lightly packed fresh cake crumbs*

¼ to ½ cup frosting

1½ to 3 teaspoons flavored coffee creamer or liqueur

2 bars (4 ounces each) 60-70% bittersweet chocolate, coarsely chopped

Crumble cake scraps until they resemble coarse crumbs.

1 Combine crumbs, frosting and creamer in medium bowl. Gently mix together until evenly blended. If mixture seems dry and doesn't hold together when pressed, add additional frosting.

2 Form mixture into 1-inch balls, rolling between palms until evenly shaped. Set onto waxed paper.

3 Carefully melt chocolate in double boiler over low heat; do not let water splash into chocolate. Or melt chocolate in glass measuring cup in microwave on MEDIUM (50%) 60 to 90 seconds. Stir; continue to microwave in 30-second intervals, stirring until chocolate has melted completely. (Reheat on MEDIUM, if necessary.)

4 Place cake ball on skewer and dip completely into chocolate. Tap skewer gently to let excess chocolate drip back into double boiler; place coated ball on waxed paper. Repeat with remaining cake balls. Let stand until chocolate cools. Store bonbons in refrigerator up to 1 week.

NOTE: Use any leftover cake you may have—frosted layer cake, cupcakes, bundt cake or snack cake—or bake any cake mix according to package directions in a 13×9-inch pan, cool completely and crumble it into a bowl. You can also use leftover cake and frosting from Chocolate Cake Milkshake on page 183. Cut about a quarter of it and crumble the cake and frosting together. You can also use half of the cake and some of the frosting from the Sprinkle Cake and Ice Cream Jars on page 173.

CHOCOLATE-COVERED ESPRESSO POPS

makes 24 pops

1 container (about 9 ounces) chocolate sprinkles

1 pint (2 cups) chocolate gelato or ice cream

1 cup chocolate-covered espresso beans, coarsely chopped*

Pop sticks or coffee stirrers

Chocolate-covered espresso beans are available in fine supermarkets and gourmet food stores.

1 Line medium baking sheet with plastic wrap. Spread chocolate sprinkles in shallow dish; set aside.

2 Scoop gelato into chilled large metal bowl. Cut in chocolate-covered espresso beans with pastry blender or two knives; fold and cut again. Repeat, working fast, until mixture is evenly incorporated.

3 Scoop 24 rounded tablespoonfuls gelato mixture into sprinkles. Gently roll into balls, turning to coat and pressing mixture evenly into gelato. Place on prepared baking sheet. Freeze 1 hour.

4 Insert sticks. Freeze 1 hour or until firm.

TIP: You can skip the pop sticks and serve the pops like frozen truffles. For longer storage, wrap the frozen pops tightly in plastic wrap and store them in a freezer food storage bag.

PARTY POPCORN

makes 6 quarts

¼ cup vegetable oil
½ cup unpopped popcorn kernels
1 teaspoon fine sea salt or popcorn salt

4 ounces almond bark, chopped
Rainbow nonpareils

1 Line two sheet pans with parchment paper.

2 Heat oil in large 6-quart saucepan over medium-high heat 1 minute. Add popcorn. Cover tightly with lid and cook 2 to 3 minutes or until popcorn slows to about 1 second between pops, carefully shaking pan occasionally. Spread popcorn on prepared sheet pans; immediately sprinkle with salt and toss gently to blend.

3 Melt almond bark according to package directions. Drizzle over popcorn; sprinkle with nonpareils. Let stand until set. Store popcorn in airtight container for a few days.

CHOCOLATE CAKE MILKSHAKE

makes 1 serving (2 cups)

1 slice (⅛ of cake) Rich Chocolate Cake (recipe follows)

½ cup milk

2 scoops vanilla ice cream (about 1 cup total)

1 Prepare and frost Rich Chocolate Cake.

2 Combine milk, ice cream and cake slice in blender; blend just until cake is incorporated but texture of shake is not completely smooth.

RICH CHOCOLATE CAKE

makes 8 to 10 servings

1 package (about 15 ounces) devil's food cake mix

1 cup cold water

1 cup mayonnaise

3 eggs

1½ containers (16 ounces each) chocolate frosting

1 Preheat oven to 350°F. Spray 2 (9-inch) round cake pans with nonstick cooking spray.

2 Beat cake mix, water, mayonnaise and eggs in large bowl with electric mixer at low speed 30 seconds. Beat at medium speed 2 minutes. Pour into prepared pans.

3 Bake about 25 minutes or until toothpick inserted into centers comes out clean. Cool in pans 10 minutes; remove to wire racks to cool completely.

4 Fill and frost cake with chocolate frosting.

TIP: Although it seems excessive to make a whole layer cake just for a milkshake, the cake is really easy and it's perfect to serve for dessert as, well, cake! And you can (and should) use leftover cake to make Cake Bonbons on page 177.

TINY TOFFEE POPS

makes 14 pops

1 pint (2 cups) chocolate ice cream
1½ cups chocolate-covered toffee chips
½ cup finely chopped blanched almonds

½ cup finely chopped milk chocolate
Pop sticks

1 Line small baking sheet with plastic wrap. Scoop 14 rounded tablespoonfuls ice cream onto prepared baking sheet. Freeze 2 hours or until firm.

2 Combine toffee chips, almonds and chocolate in shallow dish; mix well. Gently roll ice cream into balls in mixture, turning to coat and pressing mixture evenly into ice cream. Return to baking sheet.*

3 Insert sticks. Freeze 2 hours or until firm.

*If ice cream melts on baking sheet, place baking sheet and ice cream in freezer 30 minutes before continuing. If ice cream is too hard, let stand 1 to 2 minutes before rolling in mixture.

TIP: You can skip the pop sticks and serve the pops like frozen truffles. For longer storage, wrap the frozen pops tightly in plastic wrap and store them in a freezer food storage bag.

SALTED CARAMEL POPS

makes 12 pops

1 pint (2 cups) vanilla ice cream

1 cup finely chopped salted pretzel
   sticks (about 2 cups whole pretzels)

¼ cup caramel ice cream topping

Coarse salt

Pop sticks

2 ounces semisweet chocolate

1 Scoop ice cream into chilled large metal bowl. Cut in pretzels and caramel topping with pastry blender or two knives; fold and cut again. Repeat, working quickly, until mixture is evenly incorporated. Cover and freeze 1 hour.

2 Line small baking sheet with plastic wrap. Scoop 12 balls of ice cream mixture onto prepared baking sheet. Freeze 1 hour.

3 Shape ice cream into balls, if necessary. Evenly sprinkle ice cream balls with salt. Insert sticks. Freeze 1 hour or until firm.

4 Melt chocolate in top of double boiler over simmering water, stirring occasionally. Drizzle melted chocolate over pops. Freeze 30 minutes to 1 hour or until firm.

METRIC CONVERSION CHART

VOLUME MEASUREMENTS (dry)

$1/8$ teaspoon = 0.5 mL
$1/4$ teaspoon = 1 mL
$1/2$ teaspoon = 2 mL
$3/4$ teaspoon = 4 mL
1 teaspoon = 5 mL
1 tablespoon = 15 mL
2 tablespoons = 30 mL
$1/4$ cup = 60 mL
$1/3$ cup = 75 mL
$1/2$ cup = 125 mL
$2/3$ cup = 150 mL
$3/4$ cup = 175 mL
1 cup = 250 mL
2 cups = 1 pint = 500 mL
3 cups = 750 mL
4 cups = 1 quart = 1 L

VOLUME MEASUREMENTS (fluid)

1 fluid ounce (2 tablespoons) = 30 mL
4 fluid ounces ($1/2$ cup) = 125 mL
8 fluid ounces (1 cup) = 250 mL
12 fluid ounces ($1 1/2$ cups) = 375 mL
16 fluid ounces (2 cups) = 500 mL

WEIGHTS (mass)

$1/2$ ounce = 15 g
1 ounce = 30 g
3 ounces = 90 g
4 ounces = 120 g
8 ounces = 225 g
10 ounces = 285 g
12 ounces = 360 g
16 ounces = 1 pound = 450 g

DIMENSIONS

$1/16$ inch = 2 mm
$1/8$ inch = 3 mm
$1/4$ inch = 6 mm
$1/2$ inch = 1.5 cm
$3/4$ inch = 2 cm
1 inch = 2.5 cm

OVEN TEMPERATURES

250°F = 120°C
275°F = 140°C
300°F = 150°C
325°F = 160°C
350°F = 180°C
375°F = 190°C
400°F = 200°C
425°F = 220°C
450°F = 230°C

BAKING PAN SIZES

Utensil	Size in Inches/Quarts	Metric Volume	Size in Centimeters
Baking or Cake Pan (square or rectangular)	$8 \times 8 \times 2$	2 L	$20 \times 20 \times 5$
	$9 \times 9 \times 2$	2.5 L	$23 \times 23 \times 5$
	$12 \times 8 \times 2$	3 L	$30 \times 20 \times 5$
	$13 \times 9 \times 2$	3.5 L	$33 \times 23 \times 5$
Loaf Pan	$8 \times 4 \times 3$	1.5 L	$20 \times 10 \times 7$
	$9 \times 5 \times 3$	2 L	$23 \times 13 \times 7$
Round Layer Cake Pan	$8 \times 1 1/2$	1.2 L	20×4
	$9 \times 1 1/2$	1.5 L	23×4
Pie Plate	$8 \times 1 1/4$	750 mL	20×3
	$9 \times 1 1/4$	1 L	23×3
Baking Dish or Casserole	1 quart	1 L	—
	$1 1/2$ quart	1.5 L	—
	2 quart	2 L	—